GHOSTS ALONG THE BORDER

from the afterlife & more

Enjoy
Arlene S. Bice

Arlene S. Bice

Ghosts along the Border, from the afterlife & more

The accounts in this book have been researched and believed true to the best of the author's knowledge. Some of the dialogue may be paraphrased but the content reveals truth. The stories and photos have been given with written consent.

ISBN: 9781687893444

Books are available for purchase at
Amazon.com
Personally Inscribed at:
ArleneBice.com
and
Locally/signed at:
Oakley Hall Art & Antiques
119 North Main St. Warrenton, NC

PurpleStone Press

Welcome to Guest Writers

Sometimes it is best when the person who has the experience is a writer and tells their own story. In this publication there are three writers welcomed to do that. A great appreciation goes out to:

Linda Browne
Craig Hahn
Joyce Lindenmuth

Dedication

To those who have shared their experiences, so these events will not be lost or forgotten allowing us to learn from them. There is much in the unknown to educate us. First is belief. Without it nothing new comes forth. Open your minds and your heart.

Other Books by the Author:

Arcadia: Image of America Series
Bordentown
New Egypt & Plumsted Twp.
Bordentown Revisited
Bordentown Post Cards

Guy Arlen Publishing
Ghosts of Bordentown

Schiffer Publishing
Haunted Bordentown

PurpleStone Press
Major Fraser's
Life & Labyrinth
Ghostly Spirits of Warren County,
NC & Beyond
A Nosegay of Violets
Simply Put --poetry
The Afternoon Crowd – poetic narrative
Living with Ghosts

Contents

Acknowledgements

A huge appreciation goes to each person who has contributed to this book. There were many who have in different ways. Faithful readers are included in that long list. Some were encouraging by being impatient and asking me, "Is it done yet?"

A couple of the stories within were previously published in my New Jersey books, but were enlightening and unlikely to be read by readers outside of that area. So they are included here.

Introduction

Once you open yourself to all those wonderful things you don't know, they (those wonderful things you don't know) start coming to you. The unknown is often moments that we can't prove, though sometimes an outside source confirms what we just witnessed. Those moments are what you'll read about here.

My spiritual education continues to expand along with new information that comes to me in many different ways about the afterlife. Sometimes it's listening to others sharing their experiences. Reading sheds a tremendous light on knowledge. One recent book, *When Ghosts Speak* by Mary Ann Winkowski (TV *Ghost Whisperer* is based on her experiences) has taught me much about what happens immediately after a person dies. I had no clue!

Ms. Winkowski states that a person's spirit will stand at the foot of the coffin during the wake/viewing. The spirit will answer questions she (or anyone with her particular gift) will ask and also give instructions to her to give to the family. After the ceremony/celebration ends, the spirit will go to the Light and pass over.

Of course there are always the exceptions that have reasons of their own for not wanting to go to the Light. They may remain with a house, an object, or a person because of a deep love, or they may wander looking for a live body to supply them with energy so they may remain in that realm.

I highly recommend reading her book.

A section of *Ghosts Along the Border* is devoted to *Messages from the Afterlife.* The key to receiving a message from someone you love that has passed over, is to be aware. Take note of what is going on around you. It may be an object that was special to you or something you particularly shared, that keeps showing up out of the ordinary. You don't need to be psychic for this.

The messages that come may be from someone who recently passed or someone who has been gone a long while. The afterlife does not experience time as we do. Keep in mind that the bond of love is strong and is carried into the afterlife and can be reawakened when you return on your next visit to an earthly life.

An excellent book to read on how your former life still affects your present one, I suggest you read Dr. Mary Helen Hensley's book *Understanding is the New Healing.*

Please enjoy the life stories published with you in mind, to share, and to help you learn.

Arlene S. Bice

Definitions for Easier Reading

Apparition: A visible form of a ghost.

A.R.E.: Association for Research & Enlightenment.

Channeler: Channeling is the process of receiving and relaying information from an outside entity.

Clairaudience: Psychic ability to hear voices and other auditory phenomena.

Clairaudient: Also called Supranormal, hearing and receiving messages from those who have passed over.

Clairvoyant: Knowledge accessed without the use of physical senses.

Cowrie Shells: Porcelain-like sea snail shells owning mystical powers dated to ancient Egypt, also used as currency, preferred over gold, in ancient Africa.

ESP: Extra-sensory perception, beyond physical senses.

Medium: A communicator with entities in the spirit world using Tarot Cards, Cowry Shells, or other means.

Orbs: Spheres caught by camera that show entities left behind, some say they are angels.

Passed Away: Or passed or passed over. I use these terms in place of died because the spirit, or soul, doesn't die only the body does.

Portal: A doorway for spirits to enter or exit a location.

Precognition: Foresight; intuition.

Psychic Phenomena: Events that contradict physical laws suggesting the possibility of causation by mental processes.

Smudging: An age-old tribal tradition used to cleanse, creating harmony and peace, often using Sage leaves.

Synchronicity: Life-altering, meaningful, coincidental events.
Tarot Cards: Used in ancient Egypt and modern day to foretell the future.
Telepathy: Picking up another person's thoughts.
Veil: A fine layer of skin over half or all of the face at birth. It indicates a highly developed psychic perception, also called a cowl or a caul. A veil is also known as a fine curtain separating time planes.

Chapter One

messages from the afterlife

From Don Arnold Collection

A Bouquet of Roses

Devastating news can hit us hard! When a dear friend passes away unexpectedly, the shock of it is brutal news to those left behind. Marjorie Rose Powell passed away suddenly and unexpectedly on 16th February 2018.

Marjorie became a friend close enough to be considered a sister to Don Arnold and Ernie Fleming soon after they met in 2003.

Their business relationship blossomed as they agreed to manage Marjorie's artistic endeavors under the banner of "The World of Marjorie Rose Powell, the Way the World Ought to Be" at Oakley Hall Antiques & Art in Warrenton, North Carolina. Her work reflected her philosophy of life with love and generosity toward all people. She searched for the beauty in each person she met hoping to spread the love she felt.

Ms. Powell was featured in *Our State* magazine in 2007. Her work became highly sought, stirring the hearts and memories of many. Don and Ernie hosted special, private, invitation only, sneak preview events at their Marmaduke-Hawkins plantation home. Fancy hors d'oerves, appetizer samplings, and delicate desserts were arranged on silver and cut glass trays lined with lace doilies. The wines were served in crystal stemware. Guests floated throughout the rooms adorned with Marjorie's works displayed on period antique furniture. Exquisite sideboards and chests displayed her folk art paintings depicting life in North Carolina *as it ought to be.*

Marjorie, with her best friend, sister-in-law and artist, Janet Kaye Powell stayed as welcome guests with Don and Ernie during these events and many other times, too. Oakley Hall also offered Janet's work during special events. The Powell family was included in their friendship.

In all the commotion that follows the tradition of laying a dear friend to rest, with deep emotion Don opened his heart and mind to Marjorie, asking what she would like him to say in his eulogy at her funeral service. Silence was the only reply that came. He's given many eulogies, always using the same ritual. Sometimes he gets a reply, this time nothing at all. After contemplation, he decided to say what was in his heart.

He also prayed and asked for some kind of sign that he could be reassured Marjorie was in a good place.

A week following that date, Don opened his cell phone expecting it to be Ernie answering the question he had just sent, "do you want me to leave the heat on in the bathroom?" It wasn't Ernie at all. There was no one's name, no identification of caller on the cell as usual. But there *was* a picture, a beautiful bouquet of red roses and the word *love.*

Not thinking at all, he sent a message back to Ernie saying, "thanks for the roses." Ernie replied, "What roses? I didn't send you any roses!"

Then it dawned on him. It was Marjorie Rose's sign that she *was* in a happy place and it gave Don peace and contentment.

Love Never Dies

Some events in life take a while before we can share the pain of our loss even with a friend. It was now one of those times, a time to listen to my friend LaVerne, as she talked about her brother passing away suddenly and unexpectedly. They were very close growing up and remained close in their adult years even though each had family of their own.

We were seated in my home sharing a pot of Ginger-Lemon tea and the best pound cake ever. LaVerne made the cake. I made the tea. Lizzie the cat laid curled up close enough to listen in on our conversation.

She began, "When my brother passed away two years ago, his adult son took notice of a heart-shaped drop of water on the bedside table. It was puzzling. No one had been in the room. Certainly no one had brought a drink in there that might explain leaving a drop of water anywhere in the room. There was no possible explanation on how the drop of water got there or where it had come from. He was very clear about the heart shape being unmistakable. He was and still is someone who would notice and take it seriously. He even took a photo of it. There is no denying the heart shape. We're certain it's a comforting message of love from his dad.

"There were other subtle signs, too. For me, the particular passage of scripture from the bible that was read at my brother's funeral. Each time I visit his church, when I open the bible, it falls open to that very page! It's happened several times! I do not have a bookmark there so it's hard not to notice something like that.

"We were very close. When our family got together he and I would fall into a debate. The family loved it! I loved pulling interesting content from him, it was like pulling taffy. He was very intelligent, especially in biblical history."

Family and friends left behind when a loved one passes away can find comfort in a sign, sometimes very subtle, but always where a person will definitely notice it if they are aware. It can be a small thing but hugely meaningful to the one sees it.

From Linda Browne Collection

A Cardinal is a Special Comfort

written by Linda Browne

Perhaps you have read or heard some version of this little poem credited to Victoria McGovern:

May you come to find comfort in and remember:
Cardinals appear when angels are near.
So go now, sit outside and drink your tea.
Keep a look out for the little red bird —
It is there, your loved one will be.

Cardinals do have a special meaning to me which that poem expresses well. I have come to believe that these beautiful redbirds are often a spiritual messenger intended to bring comfort. Let me explain why.

Almost 20 years ago, my mother was under hospice care at home, dying from leukemia that she had fought bravely for more than a year. Mom was truly the "heart" of our family and was very concerned about the impact her illness and impending death had on all of us. Near the end, she only wanted Dad and her immediate family with her, so those of us who were able, gathered to spend time with her at our family home at Lake Gaston.

We rallied to give her whatever support we could during her last days with us. My husband and I lived only 7 miles away, so we were often there. My youngest brother Jeff and his family arrived from Virginia to spend time with her. While Jeff and his wife were in the house with Mom and Dad, I was entertaining their youngest child, my niece Jessica, who was 6 years old at the time.

As we were floating together on the lake, Jessica began asking me questions about what was happening with her grandmother. I had not had the opportunity to discuss with my brother what he had told his two children about their grandmother's illness, so I wondered how I should answer her questions. I decided that "honesty is the best policy", so when Jessica asked "Is Grandma dying?" I replied softly, "Yes, she is." Jessica followed by asking "Does it hurt to die?"

Knowing that my mother was most concerned about how her death might affect her grandchildren, I tried to think of something that might be comforting and still answer her question. I responded, "Yes, dying does hurt sometimes, but the medicine Grandma takes helps her with the pain. Grandma would want you to always remember the happy times you've had with her, not these sad times. You know how Grandma's favorite bird is the red cardinal ... let's just be happy and think of Grandma every time we see one of those pretty birds. I think Grandma would like that, don't you?"

Jessica agreed and seemed satisfied with these answers. Later, of course, I told my brother about Jessica's questions and how I answered them so that he would know what I had told her and could be prepared if there were more questions. Jeff and I shared the conversation I had with Jessica with my father and with my other three brothers, who in turn, shared with their families the idea that we should all think happy thoughts about my mother whenever we saw a cardinal. That was the beginning of the cardinal's special meaning in our family.

I actually had my first notable "cardinal visit" the very July morning my mother died. As my father was planning for my mother's funeral, he telephoned me and asked me to get in touch with the lady who was cleaning their house during the time my mom was so ill. He wanted to be sure the house would be in good order because he knew that friends and family would be coming by.

While standing by a window overlooking the lake, I dialed the cleaning lady's number and looked out while I waited for the call to be answered. You can imagine my amazement when looked toward the birdfeeder that hangs from one of our trees and saw a gorgeous red cardinal staring directly back at me! The cardinal remained there looking at me the entire time I had that phone conversation. Although tears came to my eyes, seeing that cardinal also stirred my heart and brought me great comfort. I felt so strongly that it was a message from my mother … or perhaps from God … letting me know that all was well.

After Mom died, my teenage niece Kary was able to spend most of the remainder of summer with my father. She really worried about her grandfather being alone and wanted to spend that time with him.

One weekend they made a trip to Williamsburg to visit family friends and while there, attended a church service with them. Kary later related another meaningful "cardinal sighting". At some point during that church service, the priest asked a prayer for all those loved ones who were departed. Kary said as she began to bow her head in prayer, while thinking of her grandmother, she noticed a small sort of commotion at a nearby window. There she spotted a beautiful cardinal hopping about … apparently wanting attention. Kary said that she poked her Grandpa to be sure he'd see the redbird too. They both looked at each other and just smiled.

I will conclude with one more "cardinal sighting" story that our family loves to tell. This incident happened a little over a year after my mother died. My husband Chuck and my brother Bob decided to go deer-hunting together. At the time, Bob was living out of state, so he had to pay a substantial fee for an out-of-state hunting license.

Each took positions in separate wooded areas where there was a good view of an open field where deer liked to graze. After a while, Chuck saw a big doe that was too far away for him to have a good shot, but he knew where Bob was located and figured that Bob would have the perfect shot. However, no shot was taken and Chuck was puzzled as to why not. Within a few minutes, Bob came out of the woods and returned to where Chuck was. Bob said he might as well call it a day.

Chuck asked my brother if he had seen the deer. Bob hung his head a little and said, "Yes, but I just couldn't shoot it." Chuck asked why and Bob replied "Well, I got my gun up, I sighted it in on the deer, and then I was distracted by a flash of red. I glanced down and there was a red cardinal, not 5 feet away and just staring up at me. At that moment, I knew my mother was sending me a message: please don't shoot! And so … I just couldn't do it."

Over the years, many more cardinal sightings have been reported by my family members. For me, seeing a cardinal has always brought comfort. In the beginning, there were usually a few tears too. But now, most often, seeing a redbird brings smiles and happy memories of my mother.

Three Cardinals

During my conversation with Craig Hahn about spirits and unexplained events, the subject of cardinals as messengers sort of slipped in somehow, as happens when two minds are skirting in the same direction.

Craig's mother, Jean Walker Hahn was a lifelong, admirable teacher, both as a career and later as volunteer, with a love of reading. She passed that love of reading to her children, grandchildren, and many children that she taught.

She also loved taking the children on field trips which may have been where her love of cardinals first began. Her house was full of cardinals. The entire family has long believed in cardinals being comforting messengers.

Craig began telling me about his mom.

"Mother's health had been declining the last five years. When she was diagnosed with colon cancer her health began to seriously deteriorate. In October 2016, she was in hospice, but had rallied the last ten days and was feeling fine on the 17th.

"Her bed was in the solarium where she could have the pleasure of seeing the beauty of nature at play. We five children, our mates, and her sister's daughter (Mom's goddaughter) had come together and were doing what we could to make this last time most comfortable for her. She had no more pain to endure.

"We gathered early in the morning thinking she was no longer aware or awake. I put her favorite song on to play softly, *Morning has Broken.* At exactly 7:40 a.m. as the sun broke through the trees, the sky was beginning to lighten. As soon as the music started to play, three cardinals came up to the ledge outside the window, perched there and stayed for a full three minutes. The second the song ended, they fluttered and flew away. And Mom was gone. As peaceful as possible.

We all agreed the three cardinals must have been her mother, our father, and her sister, come to help her on the way."

Mom's Angels

written by Joyce Lindenmuth

Mom had been dying by inches the last year of her life. She was intent on living as best she could, but talked often of being "exhausted," too exhausted to live this way. She was never a complainer; small strokes, and falls were becoming an ever more common occurrence.

In early July 2017, her heart just about gave up, not beating more than 25 beats per minute. She had bounced back before so a major decision was made to install a pacemaker in hopes that she would have more time, both quantity and quality. I was away in Canada at this critical juncture and my brother had to make that decision alone. I deeply appreciated the pressure he felt to decide what was best for her, as well as give me the opportunity to be with her at the end of her life. Mom did get more time, but not the quality we hoped for.

I, my brother, and Mom had explored the prospect of her death; she was not afraid to die, just not quite ready yet. She believed firmly, as do I, that our spirit lives on after death, both of us not knowing exactly what that means, but having confidence that whatever comes next will be good.

In September, Mom had her final fall. On a routine visit, minutes after I talked to her by phone, I found her on the floor of her beloved apartment, weakly calling for help, bleeding from a several cuts incurred by the fall. What made me arrive just then, when she most needed me? I had no sense of foreboding that day.

After a week-long hospital stay, her doctor wanted to discharge her to rehab the next day, Friday. She was so weak that we fought for her to stay over the weekend. As luck, or fate would have it, there were no rooms available in rehab until Monday morning. Having had experience with death and dying, and with my Mom, I was sure Mom would not be going to rehab, but rather be admitted to hospice. That Monday, it was clear to staff that she was no longer appropriate for release to anything but hospice. We had *the* conversation with her—that this looked like her final journey. As usual, she made it easy for us, accepting whatever would be coming.

On Monday, Mom was assigned to a wonderful woman doctor, an angel we had not seen before, who was filled with empathy and understanding about this delicate time. She advocated for hospice, and was instrumental in getting Mom a room in a wonderful in-patient hospice close to my brother's home in Raleigh. When shown into her spacious room, with French doors that opened out into a garden, her first words, spoken with hope and a smile were, "I like it here."

There was a rightness about this place, filling our hearts with gratitude.

The hospice doctor gave her two months; my estimate was two weeks, at most. I had fought several battles to get her to this place, and was ready to continue to advocate for her to stay in these new surroundings she liked so much. Ultimately Mom took care of that herself. Each time the staff doctor would say she might be ready to be discharged to home hospice, Mom got just a little worse, so moving her was out of the question. This hospice was truly a marvelous place. Quiet, with loving, knowledgeable staff, comfort dogs to visit, and access to the outside world, where from her bed, she was comforted by the trees and birds she had loved her whole life.

During that final week, one of the comfort dogs leapt up on her bed, and licked her arms. Mom loved it, and the dog's handler told us the dog rarely does that. I my heart I knew it was a sign the end was near.

One of Mom's favorite foods was broccoli cheese soup, which she often enjoyed at our Panera lunches. My brother brought her a cupful that last week. She savored a few bites, and ate nothing more after that.

The day Mom died, I was alone with her in her room, holding her hand, softly talking to her. She was unresponsive, but comfortable. It became clear to me that the end was imminent, and I texted my brother, Don, to come right away (a 5-minute drive). As he was getting into his car, Don became aware he was getting a psychic message from Mom.

Perplexed, he said, "Mom, it sounds like you are ready to go. If you need to go now, it's ok with me." I believe that was the exact time she took her last breath. Concurrently, two of her favorite nurses came into her room, and related that they felt a need to come to her room right then. Two of us watched her take her last breath. I felt at peace. Sad, of course, but relieved her long battle was over. And we knew she was ok with that.

Knowing that the dead will sometimes leave messages to let loved ones know they are ok, I watched for signs. Don and I and our spouses met the next day to take care of details, deciding to have lunch across the street from Mom's former home. The first thing my brother noticed was that *broccoli cheese soup* was prominently offered on the menu that day. OK!!!! We looked smilingly at each other. Message received.

I loved relating to others that story of Mom's lunchtime visit. About a week later, a large group of my friends got together for lunch in my home town. I asked the waitress, what was the soup of the day? When she replied, *broccoli cheese* we all burst out laughing, knowing she was still around. Not long after I was looking for a box to hold Mom's dishes that I wanted to bring to my home. I found one that looked perfect in the morass of my basement. As I began to reinforce the joints of the box with tape, I noticed it had held *broccoli cheese soup*! Mom was letting me know she was glad I was going to use her dishes.

One final note: I have given away some of Mom's things to others, things I liked, but would not use. Anyway, I have a friend who loves pink. Mom had three rose glass pieces that I thought my friend would like. I brought them to her and she related this story: while she was in the grocery store waiting to check out a man came up to her and asked her where he might find a soup, a cheese soup, maybe *broccoli cheese*? He had no idea why she was laughing when she pointed the way. It was a joy to hear her story confirming that Mom was delighted her glassware would go to my friend.

I miss Mom. I think of her often, as I look at the birds she loved, knowing she is flying with them; knowing she is in a happy space. It's been months since she's sent a message. My memories of her especially during the last half of her life are comforting. I send gratitude to all the angels who helped her on her final journey. I know there is a somewhere on the other side of this life that awaits all when it is time.

Pennies from Heaven

Pete began telling his story: My brother-in-law Goldy was like the big brother I never had. We were close friends who did the 'guy' stuff together. He was one of those natural mechanics being able to turn his hand to anything, make it better or fix it with ease.

After retirement, Goldy and Carol went to Florida each year for the winter. They always came to our place here in Virginia on their way home to Massachusetts in the spring, to spend some time with my wife and me.

I'd be fooling with the lawn mower trying to get it running smoothly again after sitting idle all winter. I knew I had a lot of work ahead. Or I'd be tuning up my tractor when they'd pop in. Goldy would come right over to get his hands involved. I loved it because it came so easily to him.

He was physically doing poorly the last several years of his life. They still stopped in until driving to Florida was too much for him to handle. It was painful to watch my treasured friend deteriorate. When he passed away it left me with a deep sadness that just hung inside me.

After the funeral we kept in touch and often talked with the family. Their kids were all grown and living their own lives. One or the other would tell me what happened when they had a problem to solve. Dad wasn't around to help anymore, but they would find a shiny penny nearby; sometimes on the ground, sometimes just lying in front of them. That's when the answer to their problem would pop into their minds. It was amazing, happening to each of them.

Being a skeptic it was hard to believe that Goldy was leaving pennies for them. I believed their stories, and there were several told to me, but I thought it was more coincidence than anything else. So, I just smiled and said nothing.

One spring I was working in the attic over the garage having the devil of a time running a wire that was more of a two-man job. Goldy came to mind as this was the time of year he would have been stopping in for a visit. I was thinking of him and wishing he was there to help me like he used to do. I was missing him more than usual as I tried to pull and push a wire through a hole, climbing up and down the ladders again and again, mumbling a bit.

Frustrated, I walked over to my truck to get the flashlight. Maybe the problem would reveal itself and I'd see where the wire was stuck.

As I turned away from the truck heading back to climb the ladder again, I saw a shiny penny on the ground in front of me. I picked it up and put it in my pocket, went up the ladder, tugged on the wire and it went right through! I didn't even need the flashlight!

Once I thought about it, I knew I could no longer disbelieve.

Lee and Carolyn

Lee and Carolyn have been friends with me since our children were little. The kids now have grandchildren of their own, at least mine do. They remained as friends through my turbulent years offering a quiet, stable support. If we didn't get to see each other for a year or more, when we did get together, it was as though we had never spent time away. Over those years we sat in their comfortable kitchen and discussed a wide range of subjects including life after life. The following are two incidents that happened to them.

Ah, the Sweet Scent of Remembrance

Out of three sisters, Carolyn was closest to her oldest sister, Marion. She and her husband, Lee thought so highly of Marion's husband George, that they named one of their two sons after him. When the elder George passed into spirit, they felt the loss dearly.

A few months later, about halfway through the night Carolyn woke up to the distinctive, heavy scent of aftershave. She turned over thinking Lee was in an amorous mood, only to find him sound asleep. In the morning she remembered waking during the night, recalling that Lee never wore the heavy scent George had always used. Was this a nocturnal visit? She wondered.

It wasn't long before Marion followed her husband. Now both were gone leaving Carolyn and Lee sensitive to heavy loss. About six or seven months after Marion passed over, another curious event took place.

Carolyn received what she considered a psychic message from Marion. One of the gifts Marion gave her was a music box. It sat on her dresser and had not played in five years. But at 3 a.m. in the wee hours of the night, with no provocation, the music box played its melody in crystal clear tones. The music performed from the beginning of the melody until the very end.

In the morning she checked it over. The key was under the box, not easy to get to without lifting the box first. The lever was long gone. In daylight it was difficult to wind the key without the lever. Was this another message of some sort? Perhaps Marion was letting Carolyn know that she was okay. It was a moment remembered because it never happened again.

Perhaps Marion wanted to make sure that Carolyn and Lee got the message right. A month or so after this incident, Lee woke in the middle of the night from a sound sleep. The scent of perfume permeating the air made him aware that perhaps Carolyn was enticing him. Nope. Not to be. She was sound asleep, not wearing any perfume at all.

In the morning, after talking it over, they decided to check the bottles of perfume on Carolyn's dresser. One after another she opened them and he sniffed. No. Not that one. No. Not the next one. Nope. Not that one either. After those bottles were all tested, she reached for the only one left, which was opened but never used. She brought it home after sorting Marion's house but didn't have the heart to actually use it. The pain of loss was too recent. She cracked it open and Lee said, "That's it. That's the scent I smelled last night!"

Reaching Out to Touch Someone

"When we returned from a weekend away, we stood at the answering machine jotting down the messages so we could return any calls that were needed. After a few, we came to one that was unintelligible." Carolyn said. "No problem," she continued. "Check the number it came from."

They looked and saw that it was the familiar South Jersey number that was the home phone of their dear friend Doris. They stayed close friends since high school days. But Doris passed away about a month and a half earlier.

"H-m-m-m." Carolyn told me. "First I called the number and the answering message 'out of service' came up. I called the telephone company immediately. They told me the phone numbers are always pulled right away, especially in the case where no one else lived at the address. They are not reassigned for some time."

It was puzzling but they put the incident to rest.

Years before, Carolyn and Doris had talked about life after life, discussing if there was anything to it. They were debating, not sure whether to believe it or not.

Doris was later invited to attend a séance. The evening began with the group sitting around in a circle holding hands.

The facilitator guided them, saying, "If you receive a message, pass it on because it may be for someone in the group instead of for you."

Shortly afterwards, someone said, "I'm getting the name of Francie or Francine. I see her in a wedding dress with both her hands bandaged. She said she wanted to tell them she is alright."

Doris spoke up. "That message may be for me."

Her friend's daughter in North Carolina had died in a car accident as her wedding day approached. She was buried in her wedding dress.

She called her friend to tell her that Francine sent a message and was okay. She further asked, "But I don't understand about her hands being wrapped."

Her friend replied, "Francine's hands were badly burned in the accident, so we told the funeral director to wrap them."

This experience convinced Doris of life after life. Perhaps now she was sending a message to Carolyn and Lee.

A year passed after Doris' death when the same episode happened. A phone call came from the same number.

This time Carolyn called the number back and reached a private school.

She said, "Hello, I'm Carolyn T--" to the woman who answered.

"What a coincidence, I'm Carolyn T—also." the woman answered back, remarking about their same names. Strange, thought Carolyn, but she went on to explain about the phone call they received from Doris' old telephone number.

The woman told Carolyn, "This call came in on a phone recently installed in the office. It's a number we never make *outgoing calls* on. We never give the number out. All calls coming in on that line are automatic calls, meaning they are transferred to my line and I haven't received a call on it today." She stated.

Perhaps their long-time friend is just 'reaching out to touch someone' as the old Bell telephone slogan reminded us . . . . from a place much further away.

Grief to Understanding to Joy

Wanda's son Neil was 30 years old, the owner of MisFit Art Studio; Master of Art & Design, a Reiki enthusiast, deeply spiritual, loved history, culture, meditation and so much more. A fatal car accident claimed his life too soon.

"I was so shocked that I couldn't cry." Wanda told me. "Right after the State Troopers left my home informing me of his accident I could hear and feel his presence saying 'go listen to Abraham right now.' He was right there with me!

"As time went on and our many conversations replayed in my mind, I began to think he *may have known* his life on earth would end early. He said to me more than once, 'If anything happens, don't be sad. Listen to Abraham (Hicks) on You Tube. Know that I'll come to you.' We often talked about life and life after life."

Soon Wanda began looking for signs as messages Neil was sending to her. Driving to Staples to pick up business cards, make copies of flyers Neil designed in preparation of opening her own jewelry shop and copies of Neil's obituary.

She stopped at a traffic light behind a yellow school bus where kids were fooling around in the windows, yelling and having fun. While she waited for the light to turn green her eyes just roamed around until spotting the number boldly painted on the bus. It jumped at her. **31787**. Neil was born on 3/17/87. She burst out sobbing. Just out of the blue, sobbing the tears that needed to be shed.

Wanda walked into Staples and saw on the floor, written in big letters that she never noticed before, 'DO NOT CRY.' *Now why would I notice that now when I never saw it before and I come here often,* she thought.

Grief, pain and agony filled her as tears rolled down her face. She kept attempting to do the business she came for, snapping at the girl who was assisting her in a snotty manner. The girl saw the obituary with Neil's picture and understood Wanda's temperament.

"Oh, my gosh!" she said, recognizing him. "He came in a lot and was always so nice. I did tons of copies for him and was always happy to see him. I'm so sorry." Instantly her demeanor changed to caring and helpfulness.

Wanda felt Neil close to her sending her a message about changing 'grief to understanding to joy.' Realizing the deep sorrow Wanda was suffering, the girl instantly changed from snippy to sweet. Wanda bought two Snickers bars (Neil's favorite) and gave them to the girl as a 'thank you' for her consideration. She felt so much better as she walked out the door with her bag full of what she needed . . . and a little bit of sunshine within.

It came time to clean Neil's house and remove all of his possessions. Wanda's two cousins came to help her. They scrubbed, vacuumed and cleaned for two days leaving it spotless and completely empty. A couple days later Wanda went in, knocking lightly and calling out, "I'm coming in" as was her habit, though she no longer needed to do that. She stood in the living room and there on the floor in front of the sofa was Neil's bracelet that he wore every day. It was his favorite. Wanda smiled. She knew it was another sign. Neil was okay and letting her know.

Sometimes Wanda can *feel* her son's presence standing behind her. His words would float into her ear. They are familiar to her because she knows them so well. It comforts her knowing his spirit goes on and he will be in touch with her again.

The Southwest High School of the Arts dedicated a seat in the auditorium to Neil by placing a plaque with his name. Coworkers gifted Wanda a beautiful 'throw' blanket with Neil's portrait surrounded by images that had meaning to him.

"Everything is Magic-Everything is Art" was the motto he believed and lived.

After his Homegoing Service at Coley Springs Baptist Church Neil was laid to rest in Fairview Cemetery in Warrenton, North Carolina. Wanda knows he isn't really there because she knows he will continue to visit her.

Wanda now facilitates 'Grief to Understanding to Joy' workshops to help others understand and overcome their sadness.

Jasper, American Eskimo Spitz

Some things are meant to be. When they are meant to be in a small community, it can happen a bit easier than in large cities. This is Mary's story.

"When our Animal Ark people were taking puppies up to New Jersey several years ago, they saw a Samoyed waiting to be adopted. A man back in Warren County had alerted them to look for one. Wanting to put the right dog and the right person together, they brought him back with them.

"When they got back the man said, 'I wanted a Samoyed. This dog is a Spitz. I can't take him.'

The next morning the dog went into a low-sugar fit. The veterinarian stated that he was surprised the dog was still living since he was so mal-nourished. He began working and putting some life back into him. I'm sure he recognized that the dog was of value. He continued to work on him for two days before sending him back to the shelter."

Knowing Mary had experience with American Eskimo Spitz dogs, especially the pure white ones, the shelter folks asked her to foster him until they could send him back to New Jersey or find a home for him. Mary's heart went out to him. Jasper, she named him even before she went next door to ask her 82 year old

Daddy if he would help in the fostering. Dad, otherwise known as Skip agreed. His wife Nancy sternly said, "Only until he can be sent back!"

Poor Jasper. He was so weak that he couldn't even get up to go to the bathroom outside.

"I had to carry him." Mary said. "He wouldn't eat dog food of any kind even though he was so undernourished. He's a Standard, yet only weighed 22 pounds. (Standards weigh up to 40 pounds.) I tried pampering him with Beggin' Treats, Waggin Train Jerky Tenders Treats, Gourmet Healthy Dog Treats, Pet Smart Natural Dog Treats, dry dog food, and wet dog food. No doggie foods interested him. He would sniff it and turn his nose away. I tried everything I could think of."

Skip was beginning to be attached to him. "Don't rush out to find him a home." He told her. Jasper followed him all day while Mary was at work. Soon it was time for Jasper to return to the north.

Mary asked him. "Well Dad, what do you think?" He talked it over with his wife who saw the look of affection in his eyes and said, "Okay. We can keep him."

One night after Skip let Jasper out to go to the bathroom and back in again, he headed back to bed. Just as he dozed off, Jasper gently pawed him, wanting him to follow. Thinking the dog had to go to outside again, he went toward the French doors to let him out.

Jasper went in the other direction. Skip turned around and followed him. Jasper led him to the computer room.

When Skip poked his head in, he saw the candle burning that his wife had forgotten to blow out. Jasper was a hero now, averting a possible disaster! But then American Eskimo Spitz dogs are known for being good companions, loyal to their masters and protective of them and their property. The breed began in Germany but the breed name changed when they were imported to America after World War I.

"He prefers chewing shoes to dog chew toys or Chews treats." Mary continued. "I figured he was about sixteen months old when we got him. I started him with baby food. I get up at 5 a.m. to make him the scrambled eggs he loves. He also loves chicken 'n dumplings, lasagna, baloney, turkey breast, and any kind of cheese. I coated dry dog food in cream cheese. He licked the cream cheese off and left the dog food behind. He did the same with a cheeseburger, licked the cheese off and left the burger. I buy all low-fat foods for him. It's obvious that someone hand-fed him as a puppy."

Jasper gained ten pounds in no time at all. Mary searched for his owner, knowing the dog was someone's pet who must have wandered off somehow surviving on foods from trash cans and dumpsters. He was neutered. She learned that he came from Bayonne, New Jersey.

The Port Authority guards found him. Thinking he may be a pedigree they took him to the shelter where he stayed a few days. He was moved to another shelter, then another, etc. The shelters, unable to keep him for any length of time, sent him to a private boarding kennel.

“FedEx trucks are not one of his likes. He’ll run and chase them but not other cars or trucks. He was very attentive to my parents. My mother didn’t hear well, but Jasper did. To alert her, he ran and sat by the door if someone came . He also sat patiently and waited for my mother to put his plate down.”

Skip became ill in the spring of 2011. Jasper sensed it and would not leave his side. Later, on the April day he passed away, Mary noticed a cluster of butterflies fluttering around the French doors. During the funeral a butterfly landed on the coffin and stayed there for the entire ride to the cemetery. Butterflies are known to be signs from a loved one who has passed over, letting us know he is content and at peace.

But it took Jasper much longer to find peace after his loving master was gone. He responded by totally ignoring Nancy. It took him awhile but eventually he came around and was a constant companion to her.

So Jasper was happy living on Lake Gaston, racing to the pier, jumping for the geese and just running around for the exercise he needs and having a good, healthy time being loved.

Christmas Season Brings a Visitor

The loved ones who pass away before us are often the messengers sending us guidance. Love, which is not always shown on the earth, but may be hidden in those who don't know how to be kind, it also doesn't die with the body but goes on. Hence, if we pay attention we can know those loved ones are close by, sometimes giving us messages.

Our spirit guides and angels send us messages, too. We have lots of help, but too many people are not aware of it or are afraid to believe this truth. Many of us also have visitors in spirit form which are a bit different than dreams.

Tammy tells me: I haven't slept well in a bit but I found myself sleeping very soundly the other night until the early morning hours.

We buried my husband's grandmother on St. Patrick's Day a year and a half ago. I never knew her to be a pleasant person, yet she was extremely bitter near the end. I have not missed her persona. I was completely at peace with her passing. I never thought she would need to tell me anything further.

Yet the other night, she had a very vivid conversation with me. Or rather, she very hatefully asked me, "when was the last time you have taken the boys over to see my brother-in-law?"

I couldn't remember. In the dream, I knew I was in bed, but I was also in the kitchen. That had become part of our usual *routine* when she was still earthbound. She griped. I mostly cooked her food and ignored her.

This morning she was very pointed and more chastising than normal, even for her. She was concerned about her baby sister.

Her words were ice cold. She was crystal clear when she said to me.

"You will not always be able to go see his lights if he is not around to see another Christmas. What will your last memory of him be?"

Again, I tried to ignore her. She was always relentless in saying very ugly things to me that I was just accustomed to tuning out. Needless to say, it woke me up and I didn't go back to sleep as it really got to me. Then out of the blue, around 5 p.m. later that same day, her brother-in-law called.

He asked, "Would you bring the boys over to see my Christmas tree and all my Christmas lights?"

While my husband and two little boys argued about having to go, I very adamantly made every last one of them get up and put their coats on.

We had the greatest visit!

There are times I receive warnings I hope will be wrong. This was one of those times. Sometimes, as only time will tell, they have also been spot on.

Usually, I try my best to turn it off and keep it off. I do this intentionally to keep my sanity.

My mother said *this knowing* would scare people who did not understand. My grandma said I could talk to her but not to tell anyone else (meaning especially no one at her Baptist church).

When I write, and really write, I always know when it's back on. I also know some seasons are just dark for me and I'm beyond ready for a new year as the holidays are still tremendously difficult. I am always grateful and relieved when they're over.

I do love Christmas Lights! If I leave work after dark, I often sneak by, watch and listen when music is played, too. That is my favorite few moments of holiday peace, quiet, and happy cheer. MacCallum Gardens in Chase City is also decorated and lit up from dark until 9 p.m. nightly in the Christmas season. It is a safe, quiet place to walk for inspiration. I love the gardens lit up too. When it's really cold, I prefer to sit in the car with the heater on and watch the light show. They are the only two places around I have found I can mostly stay as long as I like and no one ever bothers me.

Messages to the Author

A Message in a Visit

My son Guy drowned in a boating accident in the Delaware River on the day I came home from the hospital after having an overdue, much-needed hysterectomy. He was 24 years old. This was six years after my first born son Kenny died in a car accident. Kenny was also 24 at the time.

I stood on the beach all day and most of the night until the volunteers gave up dragging the river around 3 a.m. Devastated, but not a newcomer to death, I got through all the traditions that go with putting a loving son to rest as his entire life ran through my mind like a continuous movie.

I mourned Guy differently than I mourned Kenny because since then I had persistently sought information about life after life. I now knew Guy was truly in a better place. I likened it to sending him off to camp, where I wouldn't be seeing him but I knew he was having a good time. His painful journey on earth had been completed. I would miss him terribly.

It wasn't long before he came to *visit* me followed by many *visits*. He came mostly while I was working in the bookshop fluffing the hair behind my right ear. At first I told myself that it was my imagination. It couldn't be what I wanted it to be. But I knew it was him and was comforted. He loved to tease in earth life and apparently in the afterlife, too. That part of his personality continued.

One day a woman walked through the door of the shop and headed straight for me standing at the cash register.

"Oh, your son is standing behind you!" she exclaimed. "I'm sorry! That just popped out! I hope I haven't upset you." She explained that she was a psychic and came in seeing the crystals hanging for sale in the window, hoping I could direct her to Vicki's shop.

I just smiled and said "thank you." I told her how I always knew when he was with me but somehow hearing it from a stranger, one who was enlightened, confirmed that it definitely was not my imagination.

The playful flick of the hair behind my right ear was his message that he was still a happy kid. How could I be sad about that?

A Different Type of Message

(This incident was published in *Living with Ghosts*)

After divorce ended my unhappy 15 year marriage, my four sons came to have a different living arrangement. Our boys lived with me in Bordentown and spent summers, holidays, and weekends with their father in near-by Trenton, still in New Jersey.

Their father's girlfriend's daughter Tammy became an unofficial step-sister to my boys and was especially close to my third son Guy. She is still close with my fourth son Ralph.

My expert swimmer son Guy drowned at the age of 24 in a boating accident. Tammy was devastated! She loved him as a big brother and looked up to him as a sister would do. Youth seemed to have more difficulty in accepting death when it happens in their age group.

She and I fell into conversation about ten years later about Guy's passing. We only saw each other a few times since and then only in social situations, not any place where we might have had an intimate talk. She learned that I had *visits* from Guy after he *passed away* and determined to write to me about her experience.

"I want to tell you a few things I have never told anyone because I thought I was nuts!!" she said. "When Guy passed I was so lost. We were very close. As I am writing this, tears are flowing from my eyes; the pain of everything is so fresh. He was my brother in my heart and will remain that way forever.

"He used to yell at me for keeping my blow dryer plugged in when I left for school in the morning. I never listened to him, just told him to shut up and stop busting my chops. This was an ongoing argument with us for a long time.

"After his funeral I placed his Mass card in the frame of a 10" x 13" picture of Jesus walking through the gardens of heaven. It was placed tightly in the corner of the frame. For a week after the services, every day I came home to find my blow dryer unplugged and the Mass card was on the floor. I thought I was losing my mind to the point that I finally made my friend come over and verify that I was leaving the blow dryer plugged in and the Mass card tightly placed in the corner of the picture frame.

"When I came home that day, she came with me and witnessed the same thing that had been happening repeatedly. The Mass card was on the floor and the blow dryer unplugged. I finally got the message."

I knew he was still looking out for me, protecting me and that he had gone away but was still here.

"Okay Guy, I get it. From that day on, I have never left my blow dryer plugged in again."

Patchouli

Anne Peterson worked in a bookshop two doors from mine when we met. She became a dear friend of mine for nearly 20 years. We went to music events, book signings, museums, lectures, the theatre, and traveled out of state on occasion. She introduced me to her dad back home in St. Mary's, Elk County and invited me to spend the weekend a few times. The town is located in the mountainous area of northwestern Pennsylvania surrounded by deep, deep forests and streams that were still filled with trout. It also had, at that time, a beer spout that ran continuously free for anyone who came to the Straub distillery.

The neighborhood made for enjoyable early morning walks, up hills and down hills. Her dad's home was just a few blocks from the charming downtown area, so I made a point to walk there, too before the town woke up for the workday. It has an interesting history of predominantly Bavarian Catholic immigrants escaping persecution and buying the land ca. 1842 to live in peace.

I sat with Anne when her beloved broke her heart and when a former husband died. We shared theories, ideals, not struggles to understand life. We shared memories that made us laugh and some we cried over. When I was ill she drove the ten mile round trip from Roebling, New Jersey where she lived, to Bordentown where I lived, to go a block away to pick up some medicine for me. She was that kind of friend.

Anne helped me in my book/gift shop and was exceptional at handling the social events I hosted. We also gathered a small group of single women who hung out together on holidays and impromptu dinner parties. She was expert at choosing the exact birthday gift I would adore and those gifts from over the years are in each room of my home. Her presence is still evident even since I've changed where I live.

When I moved to North Carolina, we stayed in touch by phone. I'm not good at choosing interior colors for my house but the white walls were driving me to despair! I called Anne. She asked the color of my carpet, the layout of my rooms, and a bunch of other questions.

The furniture was familiar. She told me exactly what colors to paint my walls and it came out perfect!

Her house became my home-away-from-home when I traveled back to Bordentown twice a year. She said that when I came back to Jersey her life became exciting again, because we did things, went places, met people, and had fun.

After 8 years of my new life, she finally hopped the train south to stay and spend some time with me. I introduced her to my friends, showed her around and we just hung out together. She noted how happy and content I was, living in the forests of Warren County and decided it would suit her, too. Right then as we talked, she planned to put her house on the market as soon as she got home and move south when it sold.

The morning before she was to leave for home I let her sleep late. She was not a late sleeper, ever. I thought the country air had relaxed her. When I finally went in to wake her, she had suffered a stroke. Anne passed away a week later in Chapel Hill Hospital with her loving family around her. I cried. I still miss her.

Occasionally messages come to me from Anne. I know she is near when the scent of patchouli overwhelms me.

Being Aware is all it Takes

Moments I've written about before:

Even though I wasn't aware of it right away many obvious messages came to me after my husband Angelo passed away. It went on for several years. I connected each of them to a particular moment in our life together. *Two Ghosts Dancing* was the title I gave to an abstract painting that I bought from Mike Maugeri, the editor of the Bordentown Register News. It reminded me of the many Saturday nights that Angelo took me dancing, usually at the Elks Lodge in Bordentown. I hung it on the wall in our bedroom where I would see it every day. The next morning I found it on the floor, upright where it had fallen straight down. After saying, "I'm glad you approve of it Angelo." I picked it up and hung it right back on the nail again. This time it stayed there.

When we had ceiling fans installed Angelo insisted we have one over the dining room table. I protested that it would cool any food placed on the table and didn't like the idea of it. It was installed anyway.

Two years after Angelo passed I came down the steps early in the morning as usual. Before I placed my foot from the bottom step onto the dining room floor I noticed the ceiling fan turning. Around and around and around. *What gives?* I thought. It's January and I had not even used the fan last summer at all! Once I thought about it, I realized Angelo was sending me a message.

It became my habit on Sunday mornings to listen to the Philadelphia FM radio station that was devoted to Elvis Presley. They played some of his music that was incomplete, never released to the public, his gospel, interviews, etc. It took me back to my teen years, a happy and simple time. I turned the radios on in the kitchen, living room, and bedroom so I would get a true stereo sound as I showered and dressed moving from room to room and from upstairs to downstairs.

This one particular morning I came out of the shower and noticed the bedroom radio was turned off! *Wow,* I thought. *How did that happen?* I dressed and went downstairs. No radio played in the living room and the kitchen radio was silent! All the other electric in the apartment was undisturbed. This was eerie!

It took a while but when I began to put these all those moments together, I realized, they were more messages from Angelo. He was still tuned in! There were too many to be coincidences.

A year or two later I sold the business in preparation to move away within the next two years. It was July and very hot. I had taken a lot of inventory from my book/gift shop to the upstairs guest room-turned-into-office.

On one particular day I loaded some inventory onto Ebay. I decided to take a break and pushed some of the boxes of inventory aside. I lay down and glanced at the bookshelves built into a doorway opening. It once led to another room but was now closed off and made into a bookcase.

A summer silence filled the room. Relaxing, my eyes roamed around the room, contented and peaceful until my eyes landed on the top bookshelf where a 100-year-old book stood atilt. It lost its boards long ago, only the pages survived. As I lay gazing at it, the first page fluttered open then lay back again. That's all. No more. Nothing else. But there was no wind of any kind in that room. No breeze at all. Nothing else was disturbed. Nothing else moved. Tissue papers on the bed were dead still. The bookshelf was protected within the alcove.

I got up, stepped around the bed and stretched across the boxes piled on the floor at the base of the bookcase to see the title of the book. It was an Italian Primer, written in Italian.

Smiling to myself I said, "Angelo, you're still with me and directing me what to do."

I took the book to his daughter Rosetta that night. When I entered my office/guest room the next day to start working again, the copy machine started up on its own and printed out a blank sheet of paper! I guess I got his message right and Angelo was having some fun.

Chapter Two

spirits, ghosts, & psychic energy

Home Is Where the Spirit Is

I sat down with Craig Hahn to hear the story that surprised him as much as me when I first heard it. To get us started I asked, as I usually do,

"Is there anyone in your family or recent ancestors that is/was psychically developed?"

"Not really," he says.

When people say *not really*, I know there is more that needs scratching.

He continued. "My four siblings and I grew up in a house built in 1929 where a friendly spirit lived in the house with us. He was protective. He didn't bother us. We just knew he was there. We didn't see anything but we heard him bumping around upstairs."

In later years Craig's sister was dating a fellow (they later married). One night it got too late for him to go home so he stretched out on the leather sofa in the library room that was lined with books. He slept soundly. When he woke in the morning, sat up and stretched, he glanced at the table at the end of the sofa. A pile of 10 or 15 books were neatly stacked on the table at his feet. They weren't there when he went to sleep! And he went to sleep after everyone else was tucked in bed for their own good night's sleep.

"As recently as 10 years ago," Craig continued, "we were visiting the family home. My sister and brother-in-law were staying, too. He climbed the stairs to lie down. As he reached the landing where the stairs turned left, he glanced up at the open door to his destination, the biggest bedroom straight in front of him. This was an old house. That particular door had to be pushed and held shut with a doorstop. (Old houses settle and become quite out of square.)

Not this time! As Craig's foot topped the next step, the door slammed shut tight! He just turned left and went to the bedroom on the left. The *House Spirit* didn't want any interruption that day! We all respected the whims of our House Spirit without question."

Craig went on to talk about another experience they had with their House Spirit several years ago. His wife Donna and he, with their two children were visiting his parents for the weekend. Sunday night was time to pack up their belongings to go home.

They looked around to make sure they weren't leaving anything behind. The car was packed and checked everything was rechecked. It was time to kiss the folks good-bye until next time. They drove down the road heading for I- 85 to go back to Georgia. As they approached the Interstate, Craig reached back to get his computer bag. It wasn't there. He looked all around the car, searching. It wasn't there.

He called his Mom and Dad to say they were coming back. They left only 20 minutes earlier. He turned the car around and drove back to the house.

When they arrived at his Mom and Dad's they again retraced theirs steps, looked all around the downstairs. Everyone joined in to look in every corner, under the table and behind the sofa. No computer bag.

"Well, okay, let's go back upstairs again," he said. "The door to the bedroom we stayed in was closed. I opened it, looked around the room. No bag. At the very last second, as a last resort, I looked behind the door. There it sat. *That's weird,* I thought. *Not a place I would have put it.*

"We got safely back on the road, onto I-85 south. Near the South Carolina border was a terrible looking, serious accident. Someone driving north had driven across the road and hit a car head-on.

"Interstate 85 is number 15 on a list of 25 of the deadliest highways in the nation. The Charlotte area is the most dangerous section of the highway with the highest rates of fatal accidents according to a study completed by the GPS tracking system Teletrac Nayman. That was the very area we were driving through. The survey continued to reveal the most dangerous times was between 3 p.m. and 4 p.m.

If we had arrived at the Interstate when we planned, between 3 p.m. and 4 p.m. we probably would have been the car that was hit and lost our lives."

"Our *House Spirit* who was always looking out for us, wanted to be sure that it wasn't our car in that accident. We were immediately aware of the situation, knowing that it was our *House Spirit* who hid my computer bag."

"A cousin who is somewhat psychic has taught us to be aware, to notice moments that happen to us. We came to realize when we were being 'looked after.'"

The Arrington House

Bobbitt-Pendleton-Arrington House

*Ed. Note: Craig and Donna Hahn moved into the Bobbit-Pendleton-Arrington House in 2014. The house is dated to 1840 but a brick in the basement foundation dates to 1801. Fine-carriage maker Captain William H. Bobbitt and his wife bought the house in the 1840s. Victoria Clark Jones purchased the home in 1868. Five years later she became Mrs. Arthur Sylbert Pendleton. Their daughter Katherine married Peter Arrington. The house was featured in *Old Homes and Gardens of North Carolina* in 1939.

Craig tells his story.

When we moved into the house in Warrenton, my wife had to start her teaching job right away. So, the job of settling in came to me. I began in the back of the house in the summer kitchen that was probably attached to the house in the 20s or 30s. I was moving boxes around deciding which one to take into the other room to unpack. It was just clutter and it was just me, there by myself. Overhead is a new chandelier sparkling with four lights on it. I stood by the door and the overhead lights went off. I kind of counted one, two, three; the lights came back on. I wondered if the wires were crossed or something loose. I moved a bit and the light went off. Again, I waited and one, two, three; the light came back on.

Wait a minute, I thought. Something is going on here. I also thought this was a good time to get a few things straight in this house that we planned to make our home. A home we wanted to be comfortable in and a home that would welcome us. I started by saying, out loud:

"First of all, I want you to know that I know this is your kitchen. With your permission we just want to store some stuff here. But we know this is *your* kitchen." The light never went off by its own action again.

There is a door there to the butler's pantry. When we were going to be gone for a while, we would put the dogs in there so they would not run around and tear up the house. Our dogs are loveable but we want our house to stay loveable, too. When we came back home, the pantry door was open and the dogs were running loose through the house.

I said, "Wait a minute. What's going on in here!" After a few more times, we finally figured out that whoever was back in the pantry didn't want the dogs in there. It was time to make other arrangements for the dogs. We want everyone in the house to be content. Everyone.

We were at a gathering when I was talking to a fellow who said, "Have you met the ghost in your house yet?"

I said, "Which one. We seem to have more than one."

"The one in the kitchen," he said, smiling. He was finding it interesting that we had more than the one he knew about. Apparently our ghosts are not a new discovery. Others seem to know about them, too.

My sister-in-law who was quite up on those things, said when the lights go out like that, someone is trying to get your attention. Just talk to it. I kind of picked up on that and it worked.

Our souls, spirits are too powerful for us to be afraid. They come to check on us. That's a good thing. We need to pay attention and to be aware.

Emanuel Episcopal Church

About The Rosenwald Schools

Craig Hahn was the Executive Director of the Warren County Chamber of Commerce, writer of the *Historical Tidbits* column for the Warren Record Newspaper and an avid history and preservation enthusiast.

He was not born and raised here, but was set afire with the great local history. The county is so much better for his moving here. Craig has made a tremendous difference, even instilling that love of place in others who never gave Warren County history much thought.

Interest increased when he began writing about the Rosenwald Schools of Warren County in his *Historical Tidbits* column. This led to collecting and sometimes correcting information and photos from longtime residents who have kept them tucked away in drawers for many years.

Julius Rosenwald and Booker T. Washington partnered together to devise a plan for educating Afro-American children mainly across the South. They believed what today we call *sweat equity* would instill pride and appreciation of what it takes to get a good education for their children. The Rosenwald plan offered to pay an average of 20% – 25% of the cost.

First the community needed to secure at least a 2-acre tract of ground by donation or purchase. The purchase amount would be raised by the Afro-American community. A certified builder committed to oversee the project, needed to be in place and volunteers to do the manual labor had to be ready. Then the county could request a Rosenwald school be built.

From 1920 – 1932 Warren County residents raised $113,808 comparing to over 1 ½ million dollars today. They built 25 schools plus 27 buildings.

This was the subject of the 40-minute talk Craig was giving at the Emmanuel Episcopal Church in September 2017 as part of the lecture series of the Preservation Warrenton Program. As life would have it, Craig had benign polyps removed from his throat the day before, leaving him with a whisper of a voice that day. Ginger tea and all remedies fell away.

"Not feeling comfortable to stand in the pulpit, I found I could sit beside it and bend the microphone down to ease any strain on my voice." Craig told me.

Seventy-five people attended to hear about the remaining 21 Rosenwald Schools still standing, some restored, some in the process, and some waiting for help. The talk went well, folks enjoyed it, took lots of photos, and Craig managed with the help of the microphone.

The next day a woman got in touch with him. "Take a look at the photo I took at your lecture yesterday. It's on FaceBook."

This is why Craig waved me down two weeks later at the Harvest Festival in Warrenton.. He had a treasure to show me. The photo revealed a spirit sitting next to him and relaxing while Craig gave the background and history of the Rosenwald Schools in Warren County.

"Behind this figure is the organ. There are no windows or lights anywhere near that could reflect." He continues, "The other windows are full stained glass. No one stood or sat next to me. The figure is so casual, one leg over the other knee, leaned back in a relaxed way. I wonder if it was Julius Rosewald? Or Booker T. Washington? Or a past minister of the church? Or perhaps a long gone attendant of the church?

There was no fear, no feeling of anything sinister. It just seemed to be someone dropping in for the lecture that no one could actually see, until that digital camera showed up!"

There have been many notable members since 1821 when the idea was first mentioned to build the church. A few earlier members of the congregation once connected to the church are listed here with added information to identify them.

Thomas Bragg, Sr. built the first church. He was the father of North Carolina Governor Thomas Bragg and General Braxton Bragg of the Mexican War, War Between the States, and namesake of Fort Bragg.

In 1836 the later-famous journalist, Horace Greeley came to Warrenton to marry Mary Young Cheney, teacher at Mrs. Harriet Allen's School. She funded his first private newspaper.

In 1855 Mary Anderson Lloyd Turner was buried on the grounds of the Emmanuel Episcopal Church. The 16 year old was the daughter of US Congressman Daniel Turner and Anna Arnold Key Turner. Her grandfathers included the North Carolina Governor James Turner and Francis Scott Key, the author of our National Anthem.

Also in 1855 Jacob Holt was called in to renovate the church.

Member Katherine Pendleton Arrington was a persuasive advocate to the arts. She was responsible for art becoming part of the public school curriculum. Because of her donation to the University Chapel Hill, 18th century Person Hall was renovated and dedicated to exhibiting and teaching art. She helped establish the Mint Museum in Charlotte. A sponsor and prime force of the North Carolina Society of the Arts, she also gifted many works of art to the NC State Art Museum in Raleigh.

Take your pick. It could have been any on the list that may have dropped in to hear what the fuss was all about.

Time Carries On . . .

As a three year old child Sydney enjoyed the friendship of an *imaginary* friend Tina. They played together pleasantly for a couple of years doing all the things little girls do. Their relationship changed when Sydney moved to a new town with her family at the age of seven. Tina started to fade away. Soon thereafter, Sydney's beloved grandmother passed away. Within days, as Sydney was lying awake late one night, her grandmother appeared to coax her to go with her to the "great beyond." Sydney resisted and said *no*. Grandmother began pulling her by the arm as Sydney clung to her bedpost and refused to leave. That was the last time she saw her grandmother.

In the morning, she told her mother about the incident. Her mother became frightened because that same night her mom had a dream depicting this very scene. She had dreamed (a nightmare really) that her own recently deceased mother had visited their home in the night and attempted to take her young daughter. Even though her mom knew that Sydney's grandmother had similar psychic experiences during her lifetime, her fear was palpable and she forbade Sydney from mentioning such things ever again.

Many years later, as a grown woman Sydney had another alarming incident happen. She looked forward to visiting Monticello in Virginia. Her lineage suggested that she has a connection to the slave history and Thomas Jefferson's home in Virginia. She grew up with family stories about how her ancestor Tarleton

Woodson who was a close friend to Jefferson and who had gifted Sally Hemings and other slaves to him.

Sydney was excited to finally enter this grand home that was part of her personal history. She'd looked forward to this day as she and a friend drove the three hours distance chatting along the way. They parked the car in the lot and joined other history buffs in a tour of Monticello and its property. Their final stop on the tour was the grave markers and headstones of Jefferson, Hemings, and their relatives.

As Sydney and her friend were leaving and walked along the garden path toward the parking lot *something* grabbed the bodice of her shirt and pulled her forcefully to the ground as the words, "*Don't ever leave me again!*" were whispered firmly into her ear! Other tourists stood by speechless. Her friend tried to help her up but the *something* had a firm hold and it was several minutes before Sydney was able to come to her feet.

She was so embarrassed that they left the grounds immediately. Relaying what had happened and what had been said to her friend, they drove away wondering if this event had something to do with her family's connection to Hemings. Sydney hopes to return to Monticello someday and gain greater insight into who grabbed and spoke to her that day and why.

Hmm. Spirits are known to remain with a property. Time is never of the essence on the other side of the *veil* and cannot compare to time as we know it on earth. It isn't so strange that *someone* may have been left behind with a broken heart and still waiting for her to return to him on her own.

Sydney no longer has an *imaginary* playmate to talk to but she has developed her psychic and clairvoyant abilities over the years since. She communicates with dogs and other animals using intuition, empathy, and telepathy.

Dogs are also known to be very intuitive and perhaps psychic. When Sydney asks dogs and animals questions, they will answer her back, and often tell her their name and what's on their mind and how they are feeling. This can be done remotely. Today, Sydney has numerous clairvoyant, clairaudient, clairsentient, and other psychic experiences. She is a meditation teacher in the Yogic tradition that also does clairvoyant readings for all those seeking her counsel.

Navy Man Refuses to Leave

A Maine Story

This is the third time Cynthia has told me these stories. The first time was just casual conversation over a cup of tea. The second time I recorded and took notes but they all disappeared from my computer when I moved to Virginia. That alone was spooky.

Cynthia must have learned patience while she was in the Navy, stationed on guard duty at a Naval Survival School grounds, now closed in Maine. Her first duty called for her to trudge up a mountain that she hiked for 15 minutes to reach after leaving the paved road. She tramped through the thickly-treed Maine woods, climbing uphill to get to the building she would be occupying with another guard. Her orders were to stay on location until her orders changed.

Maine was home, born and raised, so she was used to the cold and deep snow that covered the ground. Well, maybe no one *ever* gets used to the bitter cold winters of Maine. Thoughts ran through her mind as she crunched on. She knew there would be no other movement or signs of life expected within miles and miles. Usually it was a peaceful sight. But peaceful can sometimes change to frightening.

One Friday night after she and the work mate were on duty, looking out the windows through binoculars, watching over the area, they heard a loud BANG of the door downstairs slamming shut!

"Hey Mate, did you leave that door unlocked? You know how strict the rules are for keeping it closed and locked at all times!" she said.

He swore it was closed and that he locked it behind him when he came in. Knowing she had not left it open or unlocked, she said, "Let's go check it out."

She was grinning, just knowing she had caught him in a fib. They went down the steps, one following the other and continued down the long hallway to reach the door. They found the door propped open and held open with a chair! They looked at each other, knowing something was not right, but not knowing what it was!

"I've got the keys in my pocket. Let's lockup and follow these footsteps in the snow to see who the wise guy is." As she said this, she looked down and realized the footsteps did not sink down into the snow like anybody's natural weight would have done. *It was like someone had stepped only halfway into the snow. How could that be?* She thought to herself with plenty of Maine snow personal knowledge.

She locked the door behind them and they set off, following the footsteps until they stopped in the middle of nowhere. The footprints just stopped. Hmmm.

"We'd better get back inside" she said. When they returned to their post, she gave her explanation to the rookie on duty with her.

“Some years ago an instructor was killed here. I don’t know the specifics but have heard that his spirit is still here. It shows itself now and then. I guess this was one of those times.”

Another time she and Mitchel were on duty at the same station. (They later married.) The same silence surrounded the area because there just wasn’t any other life for miles and miles. As they were tending to their routine on the upper level, they heard huge CLANG, BANG, CLATTER, RATTLE, all tinny sounds from the CRASHING of metals! It sounded like the entire galley cabinets and their contents had fallen off the walls onto the floor!

The noise was definitely coming from the galley on the ground level. They ran downstairs to find . . . . nothing. Nothing was out of place. Nothing was on the floor. Nothing had fallen off the walls. All was in good order. Dust lie on top of everything since the galley hadn’t been used for a long time. Nothing was disturbed at all, except Cynthia and Mitchel. There was not a thing to do but go back to work.

One last experience happened to her with this spirit who roamed these normally, off-limit grounds before her duty shift ended. She woke to a tapping on her shoulder when she was in bed sleeping. There was no reason for it or to get upset about. It just was. Maybe the resident spirit was saying farewell.

She accepted it knowing there was nothing to fear, just another something in life that she could not explain.

Old Souls Rising?

Cynthia and Mitchel moved to Warren County because they liked what they saw after a visit and decided to stay. They bought acreage in Sandy Creek, between farms, fields, and forests. They built a beautiful home exquisitely adorned with Cynthia's distinctive murals.

She cleared land and turned weeds into a garden that would make *Fine Gardening Magazine* readers drool with envy. Each year she expanded the garden a little more and then a little more. Cynthia is a talented artist, gardener, cook, and creative in many ways.

After a few years her mom Lucille, came to live with them in this quiet countryside area. The Maine weather had taken a toll on her health and she prospered much better in Warren County.

One afternoon while Cynthia was at the far side of the house, she heard "CYNTHIA!" being called loud and clear. She hurried to her mom's bedroom to see if she needed help.

"Yes, Mom. You called me?" she asked breathlessly from the doorway.

"No. I didn't call you."

"But I heard it, you called Cynthia!"

"Actually you know I never call you Cynthia, always Cindy." Her mom smiled at the affectionate name she called her daughter.

Hmm. That was something to think about. Cynthia thought to herself, saying nothing. She knew what she heard but who could have called her? No one else was around and it's not like she's living in the city or even has neighbors nearby.

One day while sitting at the table in the dining area, Lucille saw the shadow of someone passing by the back window. Cynthia ran out back to look. No one was there. She ran out front to look. No one was there either. No one was anywhere around the house. The dog would have notified them by barking if there was someone there. He never allows anyone on the property without a proper announcement by way of loud barking!

It happened again from time to time, they would see shadows going past the windows, like a movement but no person was around. Cynthia's paranormal talents were developed and her mom seemed to have talents of her own!

Cynthia is researching and wondering if there is a Native American burial ground nearby. The Haliwa, Tuscarora, and Saponi were a few of the Native American tribes that traveled this entire area before and during the European settlement that followed. Their Trading Path ran from central North Carolina through Warren County and into present-day Petersburg, Virginia.

There is a small cemetery of the Rose family in a stand of cedar trees near the location of the house. The earliest date is the birth of George A. Rose 1830. The last death and burial recorded is 2003. Luvenia Burchett, domestic helper died in 1896 at the age of 66. She is also buried there. When seeking names in 2006, one of the stones was unreadable and two of the stones were overturned. Three graves were marked with field rocks.

It was recorded that there was an old logging path leading to an abandoned cemetery where Revolutionary War Captain Charles Allen (b.1730 – d. 1808) 2nd NC Military rests in peace. He served from 1778 -1783 and has a government marker. It is unknown where his wife Nancy Ann Vincent Allen (b.1774 – 1816) is buried. She may be looking for him. Time is not of the essence beyond the veil.

If anyone has information, please notify me and I'll put you in contact with Cynthia.

Friends Forever

Juel lives in what is believed to be the oldest house in Norlina, probably built by the railroad man, a Mr. Vaughn. Her dad grew up in the house across the street. He was definitely intuitive. It's doubtful that her mom was. It seems to run through the family, though.

One time when Juel was ill, stretched out on the couch, not wanting to mov an inch and thinking she wished her dad was still alive to tuck her in as he used to do. It was then that she felt the quilt pulled close to her. She wondered was it him? Maybe one of her aunts looking over her?

She could *always* tell when her dad was near because he had been a cigarette smoker. She smelled that same smoke scent that always hung around him when he was alive. Finally she said aloud to his spirit, "Dad, would you please not bring that smoke scent so often? You know I can't stand it in the house."

He was listening. Sadly she experienced it rarely after that.

When she and her ex-husband Jay went apartment hunting they looked at the lower half of a house. The steps leading up to the back door were made of concrete blocks. She found a tiny little puppy living inside the hole of one of those concrete blocks.

She told the landlady, "I'll take the apartment if the puppy is conveyed along with it."

Juel named him Dave to honor the Soul and R&B singing duo popular in the 60s and 70s, Sam & Dave. The pup may have been tiny but he was the bigshot in the house! She felt like *they moved in with* Dave instead of Dave moving in with them!

Juel enjoyed paying visits with her friend in her friend's apartment. Dave was always along to play with Dickens, her friend's Great Dane. They got along famously as dear friends do. No matter the difference in size. They were gentle with each other and they were best friends.

Years later Juel and her husband decided to move into the apartment of that same friend who was vacating to live elsewhere. Dickens was no longer here.

The first night when they went to bed Juel and Dave heard the spirit of Dickens by the clicking of his toenails, walking up the 40 feet hall. They heard Dickens click, click, all the way up that long hallway, stop at the bedroom door and pause in the open doorway. Dave raised his head and looked straight at that doorway. She heard as Dickens turned around and walked back down the hall, toenails clicking all the way.

Instantly, they both were comforted that Dickens' spirit was still there in the apartment with them.

Oakley Hall Plantation House –Don Arnold Collection

The Story of Oakley Hall Continues

If you haven't read *Ghostly Spirits of Warren County & Beyond* here is some background information that will help you appreciate more recent happenings at Oakley Hall.

Reprint:

We always thought that our intentions in restoring the beauty and integrity of these homes (Ed. Note:

referring to Oakley Hall Plantation and The Inn further up the road) were so noble that the former residents, or spirits, respected our presence and didn't bother us. I think that's consistently true. We always give so much credit to the history of these spirits who were once people. We tell of their lives so they'll be honored and remembered as such. We're a connection to their existence and continuance. Why would they make us want to run away?

Renowned architect Jacob Holt built the Oakley Hall Plantation House for Dr. William J. Hawkins in 1855. He moved into it with his second wife, Lucy Norfleet Clark, sister of his deceased first wife Mary Alethea (also spelled Althea) Clark. He and Mary Alethea lived in the 1845 cottage that sits to the rear of Oakley Hall.

Earlier members of the Hawkins family served in public life, owned thousands of plantation acres, fought in the Revolutionary War, were part of the Provincial Congress, and were lawyers and governors. They've also held positions as Indian agents, senators, doctors, bankers, and railroad owners.

The Hawkins family was one of the founding families of the University of North Carolina. A member of the family sat on the Board until the late 1800s. There is an excess of 14,000 documents in the Southern Collection in Chapel Hill on the Hawkins family

In time Dr. William Joseph Hawkins was drawn to Raleigh to pursue interests in the Raleigh-Gaston Railroad and later, banking. Son Marmaduke purchased Oakley Hall from his father. End reprint.

The Folklore Interview

While Don and Ernie haven't *seen* any of the spirits living in their Oakley Hall Plantation home, The Inn (their favorite name for the Traveler's Rest/Marshall-Moore House), or their former High Point historical house, those who visit have. This doesn't mean they are not *in touch* with them. Don is particularly protective of his *unseen* residents.

Sarah Bryan, a UNC-trained folklorist for over 20 years and the Executive Director of the North Carolina Folklife Institute, called Don and Ernie to request an interview. Her brother Will Bryan, well-schooled in video and documentary production and Chief Creative Officer of Sky Farm Interactive would be working with her, making the video.

Don contacted the three children spirits by dowsing, asking if they would be content to have these representatives come to the house for the interview and record a video. Three replies came with a *yes* answer. He then moved forward wanting to have their story on record so others could learn and understand about life-after-life and spirits that stay behind. Or go on and return, however it works.

Sarah and Will came on the agreed date. Will carted all the equipment that videographers need to bring with them. There were lights and tripods, cameras and more lights to place in different locations. Sarah chatted with Don and Ernie until all was set.

She began by asking Don a question to get him started telling of their experiences. One of the lights blew out. Time out.

Will looked surprised. He noted that all equipment is checked before leaving his studio and was in top form. No problem. He had back-up bulbs and replaced the one that blew.

They again started from the beginning. Before Don got into the story, a bulb from a different light blew out. Hmm. This never happens. Will repeated his earlier performance and replaced the bulb. Next, another piece of equipment did not work, followed by something else going off. Before they completed the interview each piece of equipment had shut down.

Apparently the children had changed their mind even though they gave their permission for the interview Don knew the equipment failure was not Will's fault. The children were exercising *their* powers and maybe they were being a bit playful and educating the visitors.

Karen Comes for a Visit

"Don says, 'Our 'adopted' daughter Karen has been coming to visit and staying at Oakley Hall over many years. After our story was published in Ghostly Spirits of Warren County & Beyond her experiences have been different."

"A woman's voice calls my name, *K-a-r-e-n-* she'll say it like she wants me to come to her or maybe she just wants me to know that she is here. My husband Chuck didn't quite believe when I said they sit on the bed and touch me while I'm sleeping. Then it happened to him. They poke him, not in fun but not in a threatening way either.

"When I'm in the restroom on the second level, they'll open the door when I really want privacy. I'm not afraid at all. I know they won't hurt me. But, I think a lady in the bathroom always wants privacy, right?

I don't think I would stay in the house alone at night anymore. Something about it. . . ."

Don says, "After Christmas we were sitting around the big table in the kitchen chatting as we enjoy doing. I was in my usual chair. Karen was sitting at the opposite end of the table.

All of a sudden, without thinking first, Karen said, 'Don, there are orbs all in your hair and around your head!'

"I didn't know what to say. I wasn't sure if it was good or bad that orbs were hanging around me.

"Our psychic dog Jeff saw orbs frequently. The back porch was his domain. He loved it out there, but he also enjoyed coming into the kitchen at night when we were home. He would appear to be startled, give a funny kind of look at me. His eyes would follow them as they moved. He'd get spooked and run for the back door and stay on the porch for the rest of the evening."

"When our dear friends, artists Marjorie Rose Powell and her sister-in-law Janet, came to stay with us Janet would always get up early in the morning before Marjorie. Janet would hear children talking. She couldn't see any and knew there weren't any in the house. One time she heard a man's voice tell the girls to be quiet they were making too much noise.

"Janet was in touch with the children. They loved her and were in touch with her frequently. She loved them back. They would gather around her while she was still in the huge bed. Marjorie lay beside her sound asleep and never heard a thing. When it first occurred, Janet said to the girls, *pinch my big toe*. She said, *they did and ouch, it hurt*. So yes this was real. They said they were happy when she came to stay."

Lula has returned home. Former owners have brought a rare photograph of her. It hangs in her former bedroom.

Don asked, "Did we do the house right? " He paused, "I do feel the presence of Lula whenever I sit at the table feeling like I'm in the 19th century."

Janet and Marjorie Come for a Visit

Marmaduke had three children two girls, Janet and Lula and one boy, Barry. The girls still *live* in the house as does Marmaduke.

Apparently the children overheard Don and Ernie saying that Janet and Marjorie were coming for a visit. So they paid a visit to Janet in her home in Mt. Olive to tell her how excited they were that she was coming to their home. Marjorie never heard or saw a thing.

In the meantime, Alice Putnam came to their store, Oakley Hall Antiques in Warrenton. She had been in the store before and learned about Janet and Marjorie. Alice's *children spirits* came with her and followed

Ernie home when he left at the end of the day. They had fun playing with Marmaduke's children, all unknown to Don and Ernie.

Shortly afterwards, Alice returned to the store. While they stood near the cash register where everyone seems to gather to chat, Alice spoke up.

"I have an unusual request," she said after she told them that her *children* had paid a visit. "The *children* want to come back to play with Marmaduke's *children*."

"No," Don and Ernie said. "We don't think it is proper for us to interfere with the spirits in our house or invite anyone to disturb their realm."

"I didn't want to disappoint Alice or the *children*," Don told me. "But, I'm very protective of them."

Ed. Note. The story of Alice's children is in *Ghostly Spirits of Warren County & Beyond.* They also came to *visit* me in the middle of the night after I had accepted their invitation to their tea party. They asked permission first, were sweet, very giggly, gave me their names, which I had not known previously, and were delightfully polite. It was a first experience for me of this sort.

Spirit/Mirror: taken by great, great, granddaughter of Dr. Hawkins.

Mirrors Don't Lie. . .

Most folks today like to take pictures. It's so easy with a handy cell phone always in their pocket. Many tourists who have visited Oakley Hall have taken tons of photos as a reminder of the beautiful home it again became once it was restored by Don and Ernie. It shows the early beauty of 1855 when the renowned master carpenter, Jacob Holt built the home for Dr. William Hawkins. Some of the descendants of his and his son, Marmaduke Hawkins have returned to see the Oakley Hall of today.

As the grapevine goes, the descendants living in Charlotte told the descendants living in California that they must come and see how lovely Oakley Hall is today. So they did.

In this house where children's voices are heard but not seen, where a psychic has seen Marmaduke clutch his chest in pain, where workmen watched as a man walked out of one wall, walk across the room and through another wall; one of the visitors took a photo of the stunning mirror at the top of the stairway. . . . and saw someone **looking out of the mirror, right back at her!!!** The photo shows the image, very clearly, of a person looking out! She caught it on camera, no denying it!

Cameras are mighty objects. While the lady wandered around Oakley Hall, she wandered into the Green Room where Marmaduke spent his last moments on earth and the photo she took was full of orbs!

Lightning Strikes!

Don began to tell me about another episode of strange happenings at home.

"One morning we sat at the kitchen table, while our four small dogs, a Maltese, Shih-tzu, Yorkie, and miniature black Poodle played around on the floor. It was mid-morning and we could see through the window that the sky had instantly gone completely black. I got up to turn the light on, turned to sit down again when just as suddenly our house exploded!!!

"Torrential rains were pouring down in sheets of water outside. Inside, my chair flew into the wall and crashed to the floor. The floor, three layers deep from the kitchen being re-floored over the years, was exploding shards of wood that flew and stuck into the walls like spearheads! They flew to the ceiling! They flew everywhere! We stood paralyzed! Stunned!

"Lightning came down the chimney, hit the cast iron stove and hit the phone line. The lightning bolt followed the phone line underground through the yard and blew up the central line center in the yard. It's a large cone-like object that sat on the other side of the driveway.

"Instinct cut in and I called the fire department before I even knew what had happened. When they arrived they wanted to check throughout the house, but we declined because it would have released all the ash, cinder, and soot from the kitchen to spread all over. We didn't need that on top of everything else!

"Was it a miracle that none of us were hit by those knife-pointed shards of wood?"

Unseen Help. . .?

Don and Ernie live with ghosts. They respected the spirits that lived in their home in High Point, North Carolina even though they couldn't *see* them. Friends and guests that came to visit often *saw* them, but Don or Ernie never did.

They moved to Warren County, same state, into the former Oakley Hall Plantation after restoring the house that had deteriorated over the years when it stood empty. The spirits that remained in the house received the same respect they had shown the spirits in High Point. The spirits seem to be content and happy with that and with Don and Ernie as co-residents.

While Oakley Hall was being restored they needed a place to live, so they bought the Marshall-Moore House located up the road from Oakley Hall. When researching the old building Ernie found its history of changing hands as follows: Coler Ordinary prior to the 1770s sometimes referred to as Travelers' Rest and later Marshall's Tavern; in 1788 it was called Paschall's Ordinary; some folks referred to it as Captain Daly's; next it was named Dr. T. P. Jerman's; (by this time it had become an active plantation) then the Ridgeway Company owned it; next the partners, B. D. Moore and F. H. Cheatham, owned it; Cheatham left and for a long stretch of years from 1888 – 1960 the B. D. Moore family took ownership; Grace Wycoff Puryear bought it; the years after the sisters passed away Carl and Lee Puryear possessed it and in December of 1993 to the present Dr. Don G. Arnold and Ernest F. Fleming III acquired the property.

"We refer to it as the Inn," Don said. "It housed many people over the years coming from Europe, having purchased land from the Ridgeway Co. Many stayed at the Inn while they were waiting to claim land in the area. It's reputed to contain the oldest house in Warren County."

The original stagecoach stop was the two floor structure to the rear of the building. Pegs rather than nails were used in the construction dating it to the 1700s. A narrow staircase once wound around to the second floor where the travelers stayed, each renting space in a bed for the night, not an entire private room. The main floor was a tavern, serving all kinds of foods and beverages popular in those days. There was also a big open fireplace for cold winter nights

Stories of hauntings came to Don and Ernie but that was no problem, because they never *saw* any spirits there, either. They talked to them because physical evidence proved the house was a shared situation. (see Ghostly Spirits of Warren County NC & Beyond)

Many Warren County residents are protective of their heritage and their older buildings. Preservation is a popular pursuit in this region. In 2015 a preservation-minded couple contacted Don and Ernie to inform them that they had the original Plantation Store that had stood on the grounds of the Inn 100 years prior. They were willing to offer it for a return to its original location for One Dollar. Although Don and Ernie had to bear the expensive cost of the move and renovation, they accepted the offer.

Don reports that he and Ernie "have never agreed on anything so easily," but they had to decide where the Store would be situated on the grounds.

“Before this move begins,” Don told Ernie, “we must walk around the yard to decide where this structure should rest.”

They wondered where it sat before as they had no photos to refer to as a reference point. There was no indication anywhere to guide them.

“We picked a site, and put up ribbons to mark the exact placement it would be. When the masons started to dig the footing, they didn’t have to go very far down for the front end of the store. They quickly encountered previous stone footings exactly where we planned to place the three supports of the front entry!”

The store rolled in on a platform and fit perfectly where the earlier supports stood waiting for the last 100 years or so.

“How did we know just where to dig? Were we guided? Maybe the ghosts who still live in the Store wanted their homecoming to be on the same spot it left so long ago. We know houses and buildings have *soul*. Moments like this prove it to me,” said Don.

As with past properties and present ones owned, Don and Ernie plan to take wonderful care of the priceless structure and its *unseen* residents.

From the author's collection

Kids Playing

On a 90-degree-hot summer day near the end of July 2016, I stopped in Warrenton to drop off my *return to school* donation. The office was an oasis of welcome cool. Sterling went through the routine of asking me to sign the guest book and fill out the form. As I finished, I noticed glances between Lori and Sterling. Both had sparkles in their eyes. They were smiling like they had a secret they were holding.

"Shall we tell her?" They both said at once, grinning.

"What?" I replied, eyebrows lifting in query. A light bulb instantly lit up in my head. "You have a story for me!"

They both laughed and began telling me of their adventure from the day before. First one spoke, then the other, going back and forth until I heard the whole incident.

Sterling began, "We were delivering flyers to churches in the county. One of the stops was the Second Baptist Church in Macon. As we stood outside near the front of the church, we talked with a gentleman standing there. I looked toward the back of the property and noticed the swings in the playground area were in motion, like some kids were swinging on them. I looked around. There were no kids in sight. No breeze was stirring the air. Besides, one swing was going up while the other was swinging back. I looked over to catch Lori's eye."

"We both caught the movement at the same time." Lori continued. "The playground is in the back of the property. We had a clear view. *No one* could have been on the swing and ran away from it, without our seeing them. We parked out front and saw no kids from the time we got out of the car. No treetops were swaying; the air was as still as an average, hot July day. As we were standing there, neither one of us felt so much as even a slight breeze, let alone a wind that would move those swings.

"There are also many *things* that happen in life that are just unexplainable. When I saw those swings swinging like they were, I instantly thought of my sister. We had the *exact* same motion when we were on the swing-set, synchronizing happily, one forward, one back.

“If there was a wind, which there wasn’t, the swings would be moving wildly, going in a crazy direction, not in the orderly fashion they were doing.

“As we turned to walk back to the car, I looked toward the two little girls, I know they were girls, and quietly said, almost to myself, *have fun out there*.”

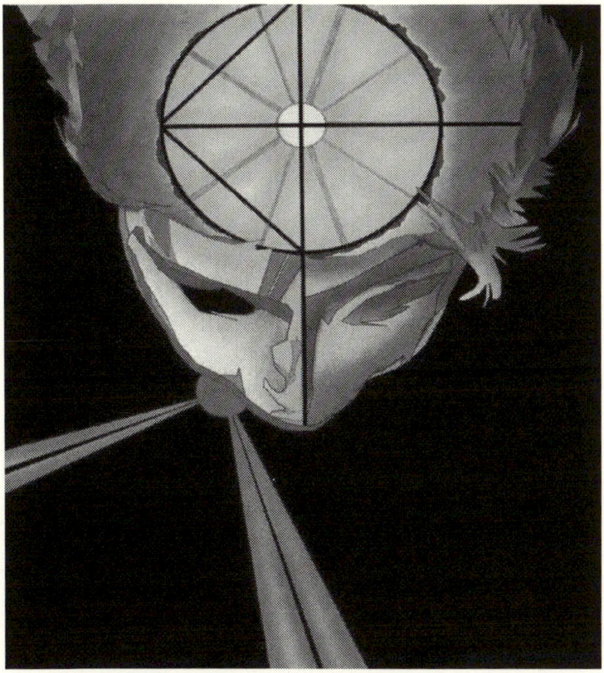

From Michael Roy Layne Collection

Heart of Stone

Michael Roy Layne and Erika met and fell in love in Boston, Massachusetts. When the time came to marry, they flew to Buenos Aires, Argentina so her family could share in the joy. While they waited for their three month residency necessary for their marriage license, they spent some time seeking spiritual places.

They met Carlos Varela and when Michael handed his business card to him, he responded to the *Cosmic Man* logo Michael created and used on each of his cards. He became full of intense curiosities and began speaking of negative and positive energies and how they enter the body.

"How did you come across this symbol?" he asked.

"I'm an artist. The image came to me in a vision while I was creating a sculpture." Michael answered smply.

The image depicted a head figure with the color blue emanating on the left side and the color red emanating the right side of the face. There was a linear progression from the left side, forming a pyramid in the center. A globe formed the nucleus in the center of the brain area completing the image. The whole figure rested within a completely black background. Varelas called it the *Crystalline Man.*

The following night Michael and Erika were introduced to Varelas' friend, a man large in height and sporting a full head of white hair. Dr. Guillermo Alfredo Terrera had authored many books on ethnology, a division of anthropology.

Michael was most interested in spiritual energy. Dr. Terrera placed before him a 3 ½ ' long box, approximately 6" deep wherein a solid smooth stone, tubular in shape, rounded on each end, larger on one end than the other. He explained that it was called *The Stone of Knowledge* and held great power. He invited Michael to inspect it and give his opinion.

Sensing that it was important not to touch the stone physically, he could still feel the power of it. Michael closed his eyes placing his right hand about an inch above it. His hand seemed to rest on a layer of energy similar to that of a Reiki master's healing energy. As he moved his hand slowly from the smaller end, he exhibited no intensity at all. As he moved to the center of the larger end the palm of his hand felt pinpoints of intense heat radiating from the stone. Michael's spirit left his body rising above the earth into the black void where he could look down on the planet earth. He saw an immense energy point emitting from the northern hemisphere on the opposite side of the earth from North America.

Then he snapped! He was again present in the living room, the moment ended! The brief, powerful, experience left him perspiring, shaking, and weak. He remembered nothing of what happened after.

Michael recovered enough by the next day that he and his bride flew back to Boston where he continued developing his writings and drawings for an exhibition to be installed at the Boston Center for the Arts.

Michael said, "Nearly a month later on April 26th while I was working, a news announcement came on the radio. There was a nuclear disaster at the Chernobyl power plant in the Ukraine, USSR! I knew instantly that my metaphysical experience in Argentina with the *Stone of Knowledge* had foretold this disaster! The location of the power plant and the extreme intensity of the hotspot was a perfect match with my experience.

"We sent a letter to Dr. Terrera reminding him of my experience in his home and its relation to the recent nuclear disaster." He continued, "Sometime later I received a newly published book and a film documentary by cinematographer and investigator,

Diego Arandojo, *Baston de Mando: Un Secreto Guardado Durante 30 Anos*, which included a description of my experience and observations with the *Stone of Knowledge*."

A Whole House Full

My friends sat at the table to chat over lunch. Memories were coming fast and happily to Julia and Jack. They inserted comments from their psychic, Pennsylvania friend Mary.

Julia began, "We have *residents* living with us from vastly different time periods. It's not surprising since the original part of the house probably dates back to the Royster Tavern/Ordinary ca. 1735. It contained six rooms. The 1830s/40s showed the touch of renown builder Jacob Holt when the front parlor and brick porch were added. More changes came along in the later Victorian period."

Houses talk to Julia and she listens. Her resume shows she wrote a newspaper column about local history and old houses under the pseudonym of Auntie Bellum. She exhibited passion when telling their stories and keeping awareness about them alive. Julia and Jack bought the Venable House in 1979 because of that passion, and passion about this house in particular. Stories are kept tucked into its walls, attic, and under the floor boards. They moved into it in 1985.

This particular area has always been a crossroad of activity possibly because it was the likeliest spot to cross the Lower Roanoke River. The Occoneechee were prominent in the area controlling the island in the center of the river where they also created a toll river crossing to continue the Great Trading Path. They acted as middlemen between the trappers of furs and deerskins and the Virginian and North Carolina Colonies.

In 1676 the Occoneechee were nearly annihilated by Nathaniel Bacon. Those who managed to escape the slaughter moved south to the Eno River near today's Hillsborough (NC). In time they joined the Saponi, Tutelo, Stenkenock, and Meipontsky tribes who had suffered the same fate of being reduced in numbers too low to maintain their own lines and losing their uniqueness. Today they are part of the esteemed Haliwa-Suponi tribe.

Clark Royster owned and operated the thriving ferry business across the Lower Roanoke River long after the Occoneechee left the area. It brought travelers to the base of the road rolling up the steep grade to the front door of his tavern. Mary *saw* the stables, a tack shop, and a grist mill. It was a large enterprise of the day. Naturally the town formed and grew around it, naming the town in his honor.

In 1835 the town regraded the road turning it to join the main road where other taverns and businesses stood. Aaron Venable bought the tavern at that time and soon added onto the original building.

"On a day when I was puttering around the house, watering potted plants and such," Julie said. "I glanced up to the window and *saw* Aaron Venable. He was bent forward with his hand across his forehead to cuff the glare, looking back at me!"

Mary stated that he was the son of Thomas Jefferson (reputed to look exactly like him including a head full of red hair) and Sally Hemings. She further commented that he was born in an election year so the child was sent to live with Jefferson's tutor T.J. Beale and perhaps reborn as Francis Venable.

Buried treasure later brought notoriety to Thomas J. Beale. He entrusted a chest to local innkeeper Robert Moriss (Morris?) in the 1820s. Moriss held the chest for 23 years before opening it. By that time, he simply gave up expecting Beale to return for it. The chest contained three cybertexts. The encrypted codes supposedly revealed the location near Montvale in Bedford County of a buried treasure. It reportedly would be worth millions by today's value.

When Jack and Julia moved into the house, they hired men to remove the tin stoves installed against the wall in each room. The upstairs bedroom also held a wood box that contained the kindling to start the fire. The men had trouble in one room.

"They pulled the tin stove away from the wall only to see it pushed back in again." Jack said. "The men attempted to move the wood kindling box. They struggled to move it away from where it sat. When they finally got it moved and turned their backs, the box seemingly of its' own ability, slid back again."

Jack chuckled and continued. "They tried again. The wood box slid back again. After a lengthy time they managed to shove the wood box up to the wall opening where the tin stove was pulled out and removed. They left the room and came back with Julia. The wood box was back in its original spot, away from the wall. No one else was there. They left the room empty. It was still empty but the box was back in its original place."

Julia just smiled and said nothing.

When Julia decided to start restoring the kitchen she chose a Williamsburg grey to replace the ugly, old gray-green on the walls set off by curtains with orange balls hanging from them. As soon as she laid the paint on the walls it turned into a Robin's Egg blue! This was NOT the color of the paint in the can!

She felt/heard a woman behind her saying, "this color is wrong for the kitchen!" Soon other women joined her in making the same comments about the color being all wrong!

They were ganging up on her and it wasn't even her color choice!

Julia turned around and said, "I don't like it either!"

Julia said, "I told my mother when she came to house-sit while Jack and I were off on an excursion.

'Don't be upset when the doors open without your help and don't bother to try to close them. It's impossible.'

As soon as the warm weather arrived, reaching a pleasant 70 degrees, the exterior doors of the house would open-automatically- on their own. It we shut them, they would just open again."

Late one night in their new, old home Jack and Julia both were jolted awake out of a sound sleep. Loud voices raised high in jovial toasts, tinkling glasses, clinking flatware sounded, and musical notes shot into the air. Someone was enjoying a boisterous party downstairs.

It took time, but Julia realized this happened on the same date year after year.

"I learned through research," she said raising her own glass of iced tea. "It was the Teamsters celebrating their annual event".

Jack spoke up. "As I left the shower one day, heading for the bedroom to dress, the wall clock lifted off the wall. It sailed by me just missing my head! This little incident was my introduction to William H. Carter; Amistead Regiment, Confederate soldier of the War Between the States. Another *resident* in our house."

Mary sat at the dining room table that same night and complained of her left leg being in pain. She kept massaging it to relieve it. At the same time Jack started feeling pain in his left leg, also massaging it to chase it away. He was wondering why it hurt since he had not bumped it or done anything to cause the pain.

Why would both of them have the same incident happen to them at the same time?

Mary revealed that their *resident* Will Carter was letting them know of his presence and letting them know of his physical condition since he was wounded in the Civil War.

During the Civil War he was shot in his right leg. The bullet went through him into his horse. The horse fell with Will's left leg pinned under it. The impact injured Will's left leg, leaving him with pains in both legs.

It was his way of letting them know he was still there, in the house he once loved, still loved so he remained.

"I *saw* Carter in the house sitting in a chair, relaxed, comfortable at last," Julia said.

Later that night the three of them sat around the fireplace. Julia began singing the old song, "*Wait for the Wagon"* and the fire flared up in recognition! The song was first published in 1851 in New Orleans but more than one person claimed credit for the melody and lyrics. In 1861 it was released as a secession Song of the South, words by G.P. Knauff.

Will Carter must have enjoyed their evening, too.

I cleared away the dishes from our Spinach Quiche and salad making room for ice cream.

Julia continued, "I *saw* a freed daughter of a freed black slave. She was sitting in a chair sewing. She communicated that the house was always for emancipation. It was also a stop on the Underground Railroad. I knew there was a secret room in the house. Also there once were tunnels through the hill to the estuary leading to the ferry. I can fill in the blanks of history that weren't written down with that knowledge.

Julia said, "Also *residents* in our house, were an older, stocky lady with her arms around children. She was apprehensive because I was coming up the stairs. I have no idea what that was about.

"I've also seen a shadowy figure. It didn't bother us, so I left it alone. Another lady often looks out the window. One lady waits for her grown up son.

"A different lady has a refined name, is an associate of the church. Her son also had an important position."

Jack's mother lived with them in Venable House until she passed away in 1992 at 87 years of age. Many of the spirits in the house went with her. A few still decided to stay behind. The house settled down a bit, but not completely.

Ice cream was the perfect ending to our lunch, but their story goes on.

About Haunted Theatres

The Colonial Center for the Performing Arts

The oldest continually operating theatre in London, England on the Covent Garden site is the Theatre Royal, Drury Lane which opened in 1663. The most famous of all its' ghosts is *The Man in Grey*. He's identified as a limping young man in a powdered wig, white ruffled shirt, tri-corner hat, and grey riding cloak.

His apparition is respected and usually seen in the upper box or breezing across the balcony before he quietly disappears through a wall. During renovations in the 1870s a completely closed-in secret room was uncovered on the other side of that wall. A skeleton with a knife sticking out of his chest was in the room. *Man in Grey*? Jealous lover? Will anyone ever know for certain?

That was long ago. But it wasn't long before *The Man in Grey* showed up again and is still showing up. Famous and not-so-famous actors, stage hands, managers, and patrons have all been witnesses. Yet this is a welcome sight because it is universally acknowledged that it accurately predicts the beginning of a long, successful run for the play.

Detective writer Gaston Leroux sets his 1910 novel about the *Phantom of the Opera* in the Palais Garnier theatre in Paris, France. The story is based on many facts. Coincidences? Myths? Hauntings?

Andrew Lloyd Webber brought this intriguing story to life again with his haunting musical of the same name in 1986. Charles Hart wrote the words and

Richard Stilgoe is also a writer of the play. Many moments have happened that cannot be explained, yet the *Phantom's* image has not been seen. But another spirit has been seen; a lady in full dress often appears at the theatre's front doors.

The pinnacle for entertainers on the road in days long gone was to play The Palace in New York City. The Palace began its life in vaudeville when Harry Houdini, Will Rogers, and Ethel Merman were spotlighted, along with and in between other superstars of the day.

Top notch plays such as *Man of La Mancha, La Cage aux Folles,* and now *Annie* graced the Palace stage.

The legendary Judy Garland was featured in her heyday and again with her grand comeback in the 1960s singing breathtaking renditions of *Over the Rainbow* and *Old Man River* among many others.

Rumor has it that a door to the orchestra pit was installed for her entrances and exits. It seems the habit formed by Miss Garland has not changed just because she died. *From time to time the orchestra members are still being graced with the presence of a rather wispy Judy Garland visiting her last great stand on the boards of The Palace.* Lucky them.

My beliefs in these short items about famous theatres and the vast number of theatres that have spirits hanging around are the result of actors who loved what they did so much that they didn't want to leave. They refused to go on to the Light where peace and love call to those who have passed away. To love that deeply says a lot about the apparitions that are spotted now and then. How can you not love and respect it?

Who knows, maybe they have gone on to the Light, and returned to be where they wanted to be.

There is also a vast amount of energy in theatres; an exchange of energy between the actor and the audience when he is on stage, plus the energy left in the costumes of other actors, energy from lights and stage equipment.

Often an actor will pick up the energy from the performer who played the same role at an earlier time. There is a lot going on when actors are on stage.

Furthermore, anyone who is familiar with the paranormal way of life, knows that renovating, restoring, changing the physical appearance of a building wakens the spirits who have been sleeping in the rafters, under the stage, or watching from the spotlights. Put yourself in their place, watching their home being rearranged. Hmmm. Time to do some research on the Colonial.

As happened to so many theatres throughout the country, the Colonial has had some tough times. As our country has weathered many storms so has the Colonial and it came out on top to be listed on the National Register of Historic Places.

The Colonial was built by Gilbert A. Saunders at a cost of $10,000. It opened its doors in 1925 to welcome musical productions, live entertainment, and vaudeville. The silent movies were featured and the talkies followed, then came the modern, first run films of later years.

The Atlantic and Danville Railroad brought top performers and actors of its time. Silent actors such as Clara Bow and Ronald Coleman gave way later to Joan Crawford, Tex Ritter, Gene Autry, Roy Rogers, Minnie Pearl, and many others appeared live as well as having their movies shown.

Retired tobacconist Henry Montgomery, Sr. eventually took over the management of the Colonial Theatre and the former Nordan Hotel. Time faded the glory of the theatre. Movies were still shown but only on weekends. Saunders' grandson, attorney and South Hill mayor, Henry "Sonny" Montgomery housed his office in the building when he managed the Colonial. At one time the post office was also located on the ground level of the theatre.

Sadly, the Colonial eventually closed its doors to movie goers. No more live performances or films would be shown.

Years passed by and the Saunders family sold the theatre for $75,000 to the South Hill Civic Center in 2001. They, in turn, donated the theatre to the South Hill Community Development Authority.

Mayor Earl. O. Horne was upfront in his vision to see the theatre brought back to life. He placed such tireless effort over the ten year period it took to bring that life back with the beautiful restoration of the Colonial Theatre that the 400 seat auditorium was named for him. He received a standing ovation at the dedication.

Inklings of apparitions being seen at the Colonial kept drifting over to me. Finally, a few people agreed to graciously tell me about incidents that have been reported at the gorgeous Colonial Center for the Performing Arts in the heart of South Hill, Virginia.

Entering into the lobby by the front doors, I glanced up at the open stairway. The level opposite the elevator doors is where a lady in a long, brown dress with a bonnet or sometimes just a bun on the back of her head has been seen. Hmmm. Actor or devoted theatre goer? Another lady, this one is blonde haired and seen in the offices on the second floor.

The apparition of a man has been seen walking across the front width of the balcony. A former mayor, who has *seen* him with his own eyes, has fondly nicknamed him Charley.

It could be Charley's steps *heard* walking across the stage when the stagehands are in the basement and no one else is in the theatre! Some performers will not go backstage alone but most of us know that theatre spirits are there out of a love of acting, not to harm anyone.

I've been told that several people have *heard,* even when no one could be *seen,* the lady singing on the third floor hallway. Anyone singing loves what they do and that's not like whistling backstage. That is forbidden!

One actor likes to take photographs and has her phone snapping away trying to catch something others cannot see. The technology of today's photo equipment can catch the formerly unseen.

While Joseph & His Technicolor Coat was being produced on stage, the Pharaoh prop was surrounded by orbs floating around his head. That's a good sign!

She continues on to tell me that the handrail going up the stairway rattles when no one is on the steps! And the handrail is solidly secure!

One day a group heard a loud crashing sound that rattled a few minds. It was upstairs and sounding serious enough to catch everyone's attention! A quick run upstairs and a thorough search turned up nothing out of place, nothing had fallen, and no one was around!

An actor quietly told me of one incident she experienced.

"In the upstairs ladies' room I saw a shadow float along the wall. I looked around to identify it. Nothing moved to cause it! As usual when these things happen, no one else was around to witness the shadow or the goose bumps on my arms. It wasn't harmful. It was unnerving . . .and interesting.

The shadow could be the lady with the long, blonde hair I saw sitting in the balcony, until I blinked," she said, "and the lady disappeared!"

Unexplained but Remembered

During the Farm Fall Festival in 2015 I set a table up with some of my books on it. The books with ghost stories usually attract people. They often have a story of their own to share with me. One fellow in particular told me about his experience in the Monumental Church on Broad Street in Richmond, Virginia. He was working in the building at night doing some major restoration work when some eerie feelings ran over him making him squirrely and uncomfortable. He still remembers it clearly.

At the turn of the eighteenth century, Richmond was a town of 10,000 people. Forty percent of those were African-Americans, some free, most were slaves. The town was divided into three wards, Jefferson, Madison and the heaviest populated Monroe where the theatre was situated. The Virginia Ratifying Convention of 1788 was held in the building on the site at the time. Such notables as Edmund Pendleton, Edmund Randolph, George Mason, Patrick Henry, John Marshall, James Madison, and James Monroe among others were in attendance.

Earlier, the property where the Monumental Church is housed, sat Quesney's Academy. It was a school that taught the latest in social dancing and entertainments of the stage. In the 1780s when Chevalier Quesney de Beaurepaire (a French officer veteran of the Revolutionary War) traveled to Europe for financial backers, the building was renovated by Thomas Wade West and his partner John Bignall into the Richmond Theatre. It burned down in January 1798.

John Marshall, Chief Justice of the United States led the fund raiser to erect a new building. The new three-story, all brick Richmond Theatre, 90'deep, 50' wide and 30' high re-opened in 1806. Plays ran several nights a week opening at 6 p.m. starting at 7 p.m. and lasting up to 5 hours.

December began the busy whirl of the social season. On the 26th, the 1811 program featured two full plays; the second one a pantomime so popular with families. Between the two plays, during the intermission, theatre goers would enjoy four short, musical presentations. The 500 capacity theatre was overfilled this night. Five hundred eighteen adult tickets and 80 children's tickets were sold which included several state legislators, a former congressman, a former senator, a bank president, two newspaper editors, and the newly elected governor George William Smith.

At approximately 10:30 as the curtain closed, the stage hand raised the candle-lit chandelier to the ceiling where 34 oil-painted-on-hemp-backdrops were hanging. The property man yelled to bring the chandelier down again but the ropes were tangled. A small fire started going unnoticed. Then, "Fire!" was shouted. Someone else said, "False alarm." Unnoticed at first, the roof caught fire. Once it caught, the fire spread rapidly!

The actors and company were able to slip out the back door, but they wandered the grounds dazed, in shock. A little known, small side door enabled the orchestra to slip out safely. Panic and chaos followed! Many, frozen with terror, stayed in their seats and died there. On the lower level people were trampled. As the flames burst, people in the second floor boxes abandoned the stairs and jumped out of the windows. Some were injured, most were not.

As smoke filled his lungs, Edmund Pendleton Jr. reacted quickly seeing the stairs blocked. He took his wife's hand leading her to jump out of the window with him. They luckily survived with minor injuries. Others on the winding stairs fell to their death when the staircase collapsed.

An African-American blacksmith slave, Gilbert Hunt had been out walking and saw the fire. He came running with a ladder and caught a dozen women jumping from windows breaking their falls and keeping them from injury.

Some survivors were severely burned, many with broken arms and legs. Heroes were made by helping others escape the flaming, scorching heat and smoke; cowards saved themselves and ran away to have this memory burned into their minds for the rest of their lives.

The fire burned so hot that there were no identifiable remains for most. Rich and poor, black and white, bound slave and masters melded into a huge heap. In total 72 people were accounted for, 54 women and 18 men. Children were also among the dead.

It was determined by a burial committee to leave the remains. A funeral procession wound through the streets of mourning Richmond on December 29. An internment ceremony at the burn site was held, officiated by Episcopal minister John Buchanan on New Year's Day. In time a memoriam of the Monumental Episcopal Church was built above the mass crypt. Robert Mills designed the church.

Two hundred years later after the theatre had been replaced by the Monumental Episcopal Church and knowing that there was no explanation for it, this workman had seen two hand prints high up on the ceiling, impossible to get to, of the building that covered the crypt of 72 people who burned to death beyond recognition. It bothers him still, wondering who put them there and how.

A Ghost in the Tropics

In 2015 I left a cold weather Warrenton (NC) when First Friday Poetry Night was over, receiving many hugs and 'safe journey' wishes as I headed out for Florida. I like driving long distance after midnight when traffic is sparse and the sun doesn't glare.

This would be nothing like my terrified journey to Florida so many years ago driving on a scary two-lane road between deep swamps and no road shoulders. That story comes later in the book. Now I was happy to be on I-95 traveling easy. My first stop was at a South Carolina rest stop where I slept solid for an hour before getting back on the road.

The interstate, even in Florida is not a road to lollygag on, so after stopping for a refreshing lunch and jumping back into heavy Saturday afternoon traffic, I managed to arrive at Mae Silver's place in Ft. Lauderdale in late afternoon. I wouldn't have recognized it as the same town I came to bi-annually when my mom lived here and my kids were little.

Mae was a writing friend who moved from California to Bordentown (NJ) at my encouragement several years ago. When she had enough of wintry snow filled streets she retired to Florida. This was a bit of reunion to refresh our friendship before I drove west to visit other friends, Laura and Pam. This was a long weekend filled with many miles. I loved racking up miles of roadway.

Ft. Lauderdale is lush with colorful flowers everywhere! Even the center city is welcoming, bountiful with brilliant colors beautifully landscaped. Mae pointed out that even the new condos being built were landscaped first. She explained that it was a definite sales point.

Soup simmering from the stove, homemade bread, and good wine complimented the long chat of old friends. We both loved talking about the writing life and memories. I was ready for sleep by 11 p.m., happy to slip into the comfortable sofa-bed. The last I heard was Mae saying something about a light. My lights were out. Sound asleep in seconds.

Someone walking around my bed, tucking my covers in, then sitting down on the edge of it woke me. I opened my eyes thinking maybe I called out in my sleep and Mae came in to check. I looked. No one there. I turned over and looked the other way. No one there either. I sat up to see no one in the room at all. Huh. I said my Prayer of Protection, closed my eyes and sank back into my deep sleep.

The early morning sun woke me. I showered; feeling refreshed I put the living room back in order. It was time. My dowsing crystal goes with me wherever I go so I brought it out and walked from room to room, except for Mae's bedroom where she still slept. I put it to work calling on ArchAngel Michael to help the spirit in the condo to find his way to the Light.

Mae had no clue that anyone was living in the apartment with her. I was prepared as I never know who I'm going to run into when I travel!

A Ghost

A ghost

that pants

and breathes

on my neck

that sends chills

running up my spine

and raises the hairs on my arms

A ghost

whispering

softly in my ear

reminding me of life

after death is a true thing,

a spirit without a body not to

be forgotten because it is not seen

A ghost

configuring

in front of me

as a misty curvy wave

a haint to be an image of terror

to some but not by others who know

and accept it with the joy of a past love

A ghost

cannot give

comfort by touch

because never does

warmth come out of a spirit

from the middle world it inhabits

yet the sight brings memories of passion

Arlene S. Bice ©

Chapter Three

synchronicity

What is the law of synchronicity? The universe sends us signals, which manifest in synchronicities. The coincidental occurrence of events and especially psychic events (such as similar thoughts in widely separated persons) that seem related but are not explained by conventional mechanisms of causality, used especially in the psychology of Carl Jung

Travel Enlightens . . .

Linda's group of five girlfriends, she along with Vivian, Joan, Gayle, and Carol get together for a week every two years choosing a different destination throughout the country. They're bonded longtime friends who have enjoyed this travel adventure for many years, afterward returning to their busy lives in the various parts of the country where each live. The in-between years they stay loosely in touch, connecting when something important has entered their lives.

Linda received an email from Vivian with a synchronicity story she knew Linda would love. It's important to know Vivian's ethnicity is Japanese-American and Joan is a flight attendant who flies internationally with Delta. When Joan arrived in Japan she made it a point to go to the Omotesando area of

Tokyo. Omotesando is the main pedestrian avenue for Harajuku and Aoyama. It is referred to as the architectural showcase of streets.

This shopper's paradise features internationally known fashion houses such as Prada, Gucci, Alexander McQueen, Louis Vuitton, and other luxury selections. Kiddy Land and Oriental Bazaar have a huge presence here. Boutiques, intimate cafes, restaurants, and bars fill the side streets (Ura-Harajuku) offering a selection to satisfy even the most demanding patron.

Joan, carrying her shopping bag of purchases was strolling along the avenue when she spotted her friend Vivian from the States among all the Japanese shopping on the avenue that day.

"Vivian!" she called out!

Vivian was stunned to hear someone calling her name! A total surprise to see Joan! Vivian had just left a store where she bought a card to send to Joan's brother-in-law Mike who was ill. What an astonishing pleasure! Who would think of running into a friend halfway around the world! It was a totally unexpected moment to happen when Vivian went with her son, daughter-in-law and her grandchildren to visit her relatives who were living in Japan.

That's synchronicity!

Siege Museum Meet-up

Several years before I had any thought of writing my great-grandfather, Addis Bice's story, it came to mind to visit Petersburg, Virginia. I had been exploring North Carolina because I moved there in '05 and wanted to know the history of the area where I lived. Mostly the visit to Petersburg came about because the name has always intrigued me; Petersburg. I've read of the charm of St. Petersburg, the town Peter the Great built out of swamp land in Russia's eighteenth century history. He created a town of art, culture and enlightenment that Russia had never known. In the 80s and early 90s I enjoyed staying in St. Petersburg, Florida when my fiancé and I visited every other winter. Again I enjoyed the history and the *feeling* of place. So it was not unusual for me to want to see Petersburg, Virginia.

I sought out the Siege Museum first. I had no idea that Addis was part of that siege in the War Between the States when he fought for the Union. I browsed at a slow pace absorbing the displays and half listening to the docent telling the story to a group of visitors. The siege history was all new to me and coming from a different viewpoint of the War than I had read.

After she finished her tour, most of the group wandered off. One couple lingered. Before long, the five of us began talking between us. The visitor,

Barbara, wound up telling me of her son's experience with a Native American brave when he was about 8 years old. It couldn't be validated so I never used it.

But the docent told me of the haunting of the Center Hill Mansion where the Bolling, Davis and Pryor families lived in different periods. Each era had a haunting story to tell. A young boy told of a pretty lady in white clothing, who he could see through, came to his bedside at night. Others reported sightings of the woman described as such in the house.

Also a man spoke of his bedcovers being pulled off his bed at night, sometimes before he got into it. He found them in the middle of the room piled on the floor. In the 1890s a woman stated that she heard melodeon music coming from the library when the house was vacant other than her self.

The most stunning story the docent repeated was the annual January 24th appearance at 7:30 pm precisely. The sound of the lower level office door opened and ghostly Civil War soldiers came marching through it with rapiers rattling as they marched up the stairs. Twenty minutes later they came down the same stairs, crossed the hallway and slammed the door as they left.

The house was built in 1823 and has been remodeled at least twice since then. (Remodeling always brings out the spirits of the long departed.) Tickets are sold every year at the visitor's center.

It's no longer a surprise when I meet people who have no idea that I write or my subjects, but they always have a story of a haunting. Even more, I had no idea that my great-grandfather spent four years of his life in and surrounding the area of Petersburg. Nor did I have any idea that someday I would be telling his story; .about his life in the Petersburg area. No wonder I longed to explore the area! It's synchronicity!

Petersburg National Battlefield

It was a lovely spring-like day in the middle of January's winter. I was driving home from Colonial Heights and spotted the huge roadside sign PETERSBURG NATIONAL BATTLEFIELD.

Thinking it was time I took a look at this place after nearly 15 years of riding by it thinking, *one day I'm going to stop there.* The day had finally arrived.

I drove off the interstate onto a wide, open road, followed directions and turned right onto Courthouse Road. From here on there was no traffic. I passed houses and fields but no other cars seemed to be on the road. Reaching Five Forks I turned right, drove to a dirt road, turned left, found a somewhat dry spot, turned around, and parked in the middle of the-now muddy-road.

The silence was heavy. I locked my car doors though there wasn't a soul in sight and had not been since I left the main road. I breathed deeply and slipped into meditation. So began the booming of cannon, the scent of graphite assaulted my nose, hoarse shouts of soldiers in battle fighting for their lives were yelling orders. I could hear the terror of the on-coming line of blue in their voices.

I opened my eyes to see the sun shining peace down on this once bloodied ground. Still, no one was in sight. I later looked at an information sheet that showed I had been sitting on the left flank of the 150 yard angle of breastworks where the men in gray uniforms were stretched in a line. General Lee's son Rooney and his men were protecting the infantry's flank. The Union could not break through. The Southerners withdrew under the darkness of that night.

My journal was near at hand so I recorded what I saw, heard, and felt before I lost the memory of it. I started the car and drove to where the five roads met, parked, walked across the street to the information stand up on the hill. While I was reading it, a big motorcycle with a big guy on it came cruising from the opposite direction. I *knew* he was going to stop. He did; parked his bike next to my car and sauntered up the hill. He wore an Australian Outback Oilskin coat that gave him the appearance of a Buffalo Soldier.

The smile came first. "You interested in the Civil War?" he asked.

We exchanged a few courtesies and comments before he continued.

"You know, I grew up not far from here, but was never taught in school about the black soldiers' participation in the war. My ancestors fought in it. There were even 20 black troops that got a special medal. . . ."

He paused to take a breath and I jumped right in, goose bumps running up and down my arms.

"Oh, I know! The medal was designed especially for them by a general who led them in battle. I know because my great-grandfather was there! He helped to train them! I also know because I just finished writing about him and his experiences. That's why I'm here--in this spot-right now."

We went on to introduce ourselves, made small talk, some about the war, some about life in general. I told him I was a writer. He said he would look for my books. We parted and went separate ways, both sated.

What are the chances, one black man from the South, one white woman from the North, descended from two men who fought here 150 years ago, meeting in this vital spot!

Being Aware

Once you become aware of synchronicity you'll find it's everywhere. It pops up in the most unexpected places. Case in point; this very morning I was working a crossword puzzle where the number 67 across clue was German physics Nobelist. Since it wasn't in any of my fields of interest I couldn't even guess at the answer. Number 67 down was "Give _____ break!" I filled in *me a* 60 down was "Sundae staple." I filled in *vanilla*. Number 55 down was "A sly animal." I filled in *fox*. So I had *Max* and the last four letters in the clue that I was sure of, were *anck*. With only two blank letters I can usually fill them in. No clue. I had no clue what they were and didn't know the answer to the remaining two down clues.

That night I started to read Beatriz Williams "The Secret Life of Violet Grant." It's a fictional account inspired by real life counterparts. A young Violet is a brilliant physicist with a philandering husband (sounds like Mileva Maric and Albert Einstein).

In books with that premise I like to read the Author's Notes first so I know how much of the book has some truth to it. In Ms. Williams' notes I read, "I can only say I wish I might have been a fly on the wall of Max Planck's drawing room during those musical evenings."

Synchronicities always amaze me!

Chapter Four

visitors from other places

Strange Sights

Sherman Johnson has seen many things in his life that others have not been privy to see. He has one foot in two different places, just as his life has been molded by growing up in two very different places in location, physical surroundings, and experiences. Part of his youth was spent in Brooklyn, New York where families and friends overflowed in close proximity to share joys and sorrows with those in the apartment across the hall or downstairs. This life gave him a solid footing in which to grow.

The other place that allowed him to spread his wings and breathe deeply, again with family and friends in arms reach, was Lincoln County, North Carolina. One of his many aunts, Mary, lived there with her husband June. He was not always a pleasant man to be around.

June was nearly seven foot tall. His needing to stoop a bit each time he walked through the doorway of the house gave him a distinctive lumbering appearance that was quickly noticeable to anyone who looked. His children liked to hide in the shadows and not be noticed when he took to drinking and that was most of the time when he was home and probably when he wasn't.

Summers were happily spent sharing daytime adventures with all his cousins. They even shared sleeping quarters which created a bond between brothers and sisters. Sherman was especially close to cousin Diane. They were like a mirror to each other, born a month apart on the same day, the 20th.

One experience stands out above the rest.

It was summer, a perfect time for riding motorcycles and June rode a big, roaring motorcycle alongside his buddies who rode big bikes, too. On a lovely day a fatal phone call came to Aunt Nellie. The police were giving her the news of the accident in nearby Charlotte.

At this same time, Sherman was watching Uncle June walk out of the bathroom across the hall, ducking his head as he always had to do, lumbering down the hall. With eyes wide with disbelief, and mouth dropped open, he looked back across the room to Diane. She returned his stare and nodded, *yes*. She had *seen* the same thing Sherman *saw* before it dissolved like a puff of smoke in the wind.

Aunt Ida, who Sherman adored, used to tell scary stories of things that she was familiar with. Like the time she was out with her gentleman friend. As they were passing by the cemetery, a lady was walking along the roadside. Her companion slowed the car, coming to a stop to ask if she needed help. The lady turned her head to face him. He and Ida saw two eyes glowing like eerie green flashlights. In only seconds, they were outta there!

Sherman didn't need Aunt Ida's stories; he saw scary things of his own. He was 16 when he saw a man (was it a man?) with taut skin like a burn victim all crinkly and wrinkled, like the hide of an elephant. There was no neck, just this huge bullet shaped, bald head sitting atop wide shoulders. His coat appeared to be a funny looking trench coat hanging down awkwardly. One leg dragged behind the other as he climbed the hill with much effort making a weird, scuffling sound. He didn't stop to enquire if help was needed. But he didn't forget it either.

Sixteen was a notable age. He was driving to Mt. Holly one night to pick up his date. The road came to a 'T' where he needed to make a right or left turn. As he sat at the stop sign, he glanced across the road to the wide open field where the biggest spotlight he ever saw, lit up the entire area. Only it wasn't a spotlight. At first he thought it was *Snoopy*, the Charlotte news helicopter, so he wound down the window to reveal no sound at all. It was as quiet as a church in silent prayer.

Mesmerized, his eyes glued to that field, he watched the light retract in chunks, first the lowest section of light seemed to be absorbed upward. The second chunk of light disappeared, then the third. He couldn't move away from what he was seeing. His breath had stopped without realizing it. Shock! He was in shock at what he saw! What was this thing? After all the light was retracted, blinking red lights lit up around the outer perimeter to take off. Possible or not! It did!

Sherman wasn't the only witness. The next day the local newspaper displayed a grainy picture of this object that so fascinated him. They didn't know what it was, either.

Leaving his teen years behind doesn't mean his odd experiences stopped. A few years ago in midsummer, a couple of guy friends rode their bicycles up Highway 401 from the Sulphur Springs area. They brought their wine skins (pouches) with them to drink with their lunch. Following an enjoyable few hours the grueling, ribbon-candy-road ride to get back home was overwhelming. Sherman, being a good guy, offered to take them home, tossing their bikes into the back of his pick-up at 4:00 in the afternoon.

When they reached the Sulphur Springs area, they saw a huge, brilliant-white-light, a perfectly round sphere hanging in a clear Carolina blue sky. No clouds to interfere on this bright, sunny, summer day. The brilliance of the sphere stood out from the brightness of the day.

They watched, stunned silent, as the perfect sphere elongated to an enormous, glistening oval, then closing up horizontally into itself, disappearing in front of their very eyes.

The Carolina blue sky became empty.

No More Denials

UFOs can no longer be denied! ETs are obviously not going to hurt us humans or they would have attended to that a long time ago. Not only have they been seen by many reliable people but they have also interacted with humans. I heard Chris Bledsoe speak to my group of interested friends about a spaceship that landed on his rural property in North Carolina. It gave me great comfort with a bit of insight to these individuals.

On 21 April 1957, more than 50 years ago an Unidentified Flying Object set down in South Hill, Virginia on E. Ferrell Street in the area where the post office is today. It was reported in the South Hill Enterprise that the manager of the Mobile Chemical Co. plant in South Hill, Cliff Crowder, saw it lift off after hesitating for five seconds in front of his car, as he was driving home from work. He flicked his high beams on to see the 20' high, 15'wide, shiny metal tank-like object with three legs more clearly. Immediately, white flames burst, spewing out of the bottom of it like a thousand flash bulbs going off at once as it took off. Many people reassured those who asked, that Cliff Crowder was a highly respected man. If he said he saw this UFO, then it can be taken as fact.

Then-Police Chief of South Hill Gilbert Tolbert and patrolman Billy Murphy were at the scene at 9 p.m. to investigate. The investigating officers found four half-inch holes in the road with a two-and-a-half foot burn mark in the middle of them. Later, assistant director of the National Investigations Committee on Aerial Phenomenon, Gordon Lore and Air Force investigator William T. Powers also came to investigate. Local, photographer Robert L. Harris took photos to validate the scene and the investigation. His photos were also published in several magazines and newspapers.

Members of the Chapel Hill Astrological and Observational Society partnered with Mecklenburg County Tourism and the Town of South Hill to host "Close Encounters: 50th Anniversary of South Hill's UFO Landing" on 21 April 2017. The event would let people know that the UFO incident has not been forgotten. Unfortunately the event was rained out.

The Wonders of Youth

One night many years ago in California, three boys were camping out, as they often liked to do. Also as boys do, they had an experience.

Chuck and his friend plus his friend's little brother Buddy camped out one night. They lay on the ground to scan the stars and talk about the heavens. As they were studying the sky they saw a *something* dart across the dark sky, to the left, zigzag to the right, and jet in a different direction! It was moving and they were absolutely certain it was a UFO! Excitement bubbled up as they discussed it between themselves before they finally dozed off and fell asleep.

The next morning when they woke, his friend's brother was gone! They looked all around and couldn't find him! Alarm bells went off in their heads at the same time! What were they going to tell his parents! The UFO! It must have been the UFO! They must have landed and taken him away without ever waking them!

They stumbled around, wondering what to do next, almost in a panic, when suddenly Buddy's head appeared over the edge of the drop-off. He had rolled over the edge and down the hill in his sleep, never woke up until this moment in the morning.

They were sure thankful and happy that Buddy was still with them, but they still, to this day, believe that all three of them saw a UFO!

Chapter Five

when the veil drops

California Highway

This documented experience came to me by way of a friend.

Verne, a California friend, one who has his feet planted solidly on the ground and knowing that I don't, called to tell of this unexplainable experience.

"I've got a strange car story for you. I was living and working in Anaheim, California. I had a job up in the northern part of Orange County. I was driving on the freeway about 4:30 in the morning heading up to go to my job. I was in the number 3 lane with a car moving slow ahead of me. He was probably going around 35 miles per hour. It was an old model car probably from the late 30s or 40s. The taillights were real dim looking more brown than red.

I moved over into the next lane to pass. I drove passed it and glanced in my mirror to go back into lane 3 again. The car was gone! Alarmed, I pulled over to the shoulder, stopped the car, got out, and looked down the freeway I just came from. There was no car in sight! There was no place that car could have gone. There were no exits. No turn offs.

I could see all the way down the road and it just was not there! Gone! If I didn't notice the difference in the taillights I wouldn't have taken special notice.
Source: Darkness Radio Encore - October 24, 2016

In Mid-Afternoon?

(published in *A Nosegay of Violets)*

The first year after I moved to North Carolina in 2005 was like no other. I was making my way in new territory, where I had never been or lived before, living in the woods alone and loving it. Didn't know a soul here.

I'd had several minor metaphysical experiences, perhaps because I was open to them and had the peace to recognize them when they happened. I was not overloaded with work, problems, or activities that I enjoyed but may have kept me from being in touch with my inner self and those who wanted to get my attention.

It didn't last. My eldest brother Albert called me from Puerto Rico where he had lived for 50 years. He told me his lungs were shot, he didn't have long to live and he wanted to come home to the States. We stayed in touch over the years with letters and I'd been to Puerto Rico for several visits and at one time planned to live there.

On an afternoon that followed, I had been reading in my wing chair as was my routine, making up for the years when I couldn't. I dozed off till a loud voice woke me up.

"Yes, I'm here!" I answered before realizing that I was the only person in the room. The girls (my psychic cats) came out from under the chair and looked at me with that *don't you know by now, what that is*? Someone was trying to get my attention. At that moment I remembered the last instructions my mother gave me before she passed away. "You are the link between your two brothers. Keep in contact."

I flew down to bring him back with me in November. Months later on the 30th of March, we were driving north out of Raleigh. We stopped at a traffic light on a section of Highway 401 where it is four lanes wide, divided by a left turn lane. I was in the right hand lane; an SUV, much larger than mine, was to my left in its own lane. Suddenly, a car full of teenagers pulled between us, straddling the line. I looked, shocked! There was no crash, no sound of metal crunched and absolutely no room for that car to be there! Yet I *saw* the kids laughing, carefree and enjoying themselves. My brother, who has had psychic moments of his own over the years, was looking the other way, out his window and saw nothing.

The light changed and I pulled away to let the other car deal with it. But he pulled away, too. I didn't get it. How could that be? And how could they be laughing in such a situation? I just didn't understand. I thought about this over and over. I even talked to a few people that I was sure would not look at me askew or wonder if I was a nut. At the time no one had an answer for me.

I knew there wasn't more than three to four feet of space between the SUV and me. There was not enough room for the full size car I *saw*. At that point I thought perhaps my car was in a bubble, shielded by one of my spirit guides. I really stretched my imagination trying to understand what I saw. I had experienced other instances on the road when I knew a spirit or angel had protected me. Maybe that was a new one

Then I analyzed and remembered details. The teens' dress and haircuts were from the late 1930s to early 1940s period that I had seen in movies. The driver's hair had neatness about it, cut close up the back, as if with electric clippers. The collar of his shirt was spread wide open like I had seen in pictures of Albert born in the 30s. The girls' hairstyles were also from that period and had ribbons or kerchiefs tied around them. Their car sat high, not as high as the larger SUV. Their laughing was joyous not sarcastic.

It took some time of this *happening* to ferment in the back of my mind (It's always with me if not prominently so.) Then I realized, as if someone put the answer into my head. The unseen veil that hangs between layers of time, dropped. I *saw* into an earlier time period! That's why there was no crash, no alarm on their faces, no scratches, or dents on my car. I saw innocent teens out for an afternoon of fun, enjoying every moment together. It was a type of psychic moment that I had not experienced before.

Off I-85

A few years ago Sharon and I planned our excursion to the Rhine Center in Durham, North Carolina. She doesn't like to drive in heavy traffic so we agreed to meet at motel parking lot off of I-85, leave her bug and I'd drive. We had done this before when we were traveling in the same direction to the same place.

This particular event was a Friday night at the Rhine Research Center, a non-profit research and educational organization for scientific study of parapsychology. They explore the mind beyond the five senses. Although I had been to lectures and films there, it was my first time at the featured 'games' night. We both desired to expand our knowledge of the paranormal. Games were a fun way of examining our psychic abilities.

There were five games going on with a small group in each game and then we switched and went on to the next so everyone got a chance at each game. The first one I went to was 'remote viewing.' I did very well with looking at a box and drawing what was inside. I drew the shape of the item though I didn't know what it was. It turned out to be an old fashioned hand stamp that would be used to stamp a seal on papers like a notary would use. A deck of cards followed where we were to write down the markings on certain cards. I failed badly. The instructor said it was below normal indicating that I was subconsciously blocking my abilities. I couldn't bend any spoons with my mind. Several others did. Mentally I barely moved the hands on the clock and I did average on seeing how many pips were coming up on the next throw of a die. It was a fun evening and experiment. The psychic talents of others impressed me.

We drove back to the motel, Sharon got into her bug and I waited till she was on her way, pulling out behind her. She pulled out of the parking lot and turned left onto the road and took off. I pulled out of the parking lot up to the road and stopped, stunned! I didn't recognize where I was! The gas station wasn't across the street where it was when I drove in! I instantly lost my bearings! Confused! It was a simple thing to turn left onto the road and right onto I-85. Instead I drove across the road and saw an old-time market on the right where the gas station should have been! I drove a wee bit further and there was a forest there so I did my famous U-turn (I personally love U-turns) drove back the very short distance to the road, turned right and everything was as it was supposed to be. Thankfully.

As my usual, hiding habit, I told no one, afraid someone would say it was my age, or I was befuddled, or some other silly explanation that would annoy me. Again, as usual I thought about it and thought about it. It finally dawned on me as I had the experience, at least once before, in Raleigh. The veil dropped and I had driven into a time past. I'm glad it was brief.

Chapter Six

someone watches over me

Faith

Lori's Story

We sat in the cool office chatting easily. My sensors felt like Lori had something to tell me. Since we had been talking about things we can't see or sometimes cannot explain and as a matter of course, I inquired if there were any psychically developed members in her family, presently or in the past. That's just unofficial research on seeking to find lineages of the psychic in families.

"No," she replied. "But I may have had a *near death experience.*

Fifteen years ago, and I've only ever mentioned this to one person, I was on Lake Gaston with family and friends, in my brother-in-law's boat. Securing the straps on my lifejacket, I asked, "What would happen if I jumped into the water?" I never learned how to swim but I love the water and it looked so inviting. Would the life jacket hold me above the water?"

"Yes," he replied.

So she did. She jumped right in . . .and went down, down, down.

"Instantly, I saw and was mesmerized by flashes of my life. Happy moments. Scenes lit up from behind, flashing here, and there, and over there. I was calm, no gasping for breath. It was peaceful, serene, no panic. I wasn't even filling up with water like you'd think I would. I then floated up to the surface and popped out of the water, head up without even a sputter.

When I was back in the boat, I said to my brother-in-law "I feel fine even though I was under the water for so long."

He said, "You weren't under for even 30 seconds. You went under and came right back up."

I thought, 'I couldn't have. I saw all those scenes of my life. It must have taken time. How could that be?

"When something like that happens, it changes you. I always loved God, but my faith went deeper. I really try harder to look for the good in people. That's what I do and I love all that I do. Part of my working with young couples, helping them sort things, to see their anger so they can work it out. I want them to appreciate life.

" I'm not afraid of death. I believe in life after death and it's wonderful, uplifting. My strong faith continues to get stronger. I have fearful moments, but they wash away. I'm not afraid to step out and take risks. My faith sustains me.

"From time to time, I'll go to one church or another, just to visit. Once a woman came up to me, looked me straight in the eye and said, "You're a prophet." I didn't know what to say. The exact same thing happened in another church. Twice now, I've been told that I am a prophet."

Lori didn't know how to reply to that. Obviously, these people *saw* something in her that she may be unaware of.
"I just love helping people," she said.

An Angel, for Sure

LaVerne's Story

"There is no need to write down one experience that I had, years ago when I lived in Baltimore. It will stay in my mind as long as I live! I had been out with friends to a cabaret. Those dances usually ended around 2 a.m. From there we would all head to someone's house for a nightcap or a bite to eat. It was a routine that we all enjoyed.

"That night went along as usual. Nothing different. I left my friends' house about 4 a.m., by myself and headed home. It's what I did dozens of times. I didn't live far away. Thoughts of the fun night were running through my mind. We drank and danced, drank and danced some more. In between we told stories and laughed at our own jokes.

"We were just having fun. Though, I *was* tired. My eyelids drooped. I dozed. I jerked awake just in time!

"My foot was on the brake! I don't remember putting it there! A telephone pole was right in front of my car! Someone (an angel?) stopped my car before I hit that pole! A half block from my apartment and surely I would have been killed!"

The Third Man

There have been many stories reported over the years about someone at the life-saving scene, who instantly disappeared from view. The internet now shows accident photos caught on cell phones where there was someone helping at the scene. Yet that someone went *poof* and disappeared instantly as soon as help arrived. Ron DeFrancesco related how the smoke and fire forced him to lie down in the stairwell of the South Tower when *someone* grasped his hand and led him through the smoke from the 84th floor. He was the last person to leave that building before it collapsed on 9/11.

In the spring of 1983 James Sevigny and friend Richard Whitmire were climbing in the Canadian Rockies near Lake Louise, Alberta when an avalanche swept them 2,000 feet. When Sevigny regained consciousness he was confused and didn't know where he was. He suffered a broken arm, scapula, ribs, nose, teeth, and soaked in blood. At one time he began to doze feeling the nearness of death and would succumb to it. An *invisible, physical being* communicated to him not to give up, he had to survive. Three cross-country skiers happened to hear him call for help.

His friend did not survive.

In 1933 a British explorer, Frank Smyth attempted to be the first to climb the summit of Mt. Everest. He didn't make it. He later wrote in his diary that at one time on his assent he reached into his pocket for some cake, broke it in half to share with his companion. When he turned, he found he was alone. Yet, he knew he had not been alone. He just couldn't *see* who was with him.

A hundred thousand people waited in darkness on the airfield in Paris, scanning the skies for the sight of Charles Lindbergh in his "Spirit of St. Louis" plane on 20 May 1927. He became famous when such an incident happened to help him survive the 3600 mile non-stop flight between New York and Paris in a challenge by Raymond Ortieg who offered a $25,000 prize. That amount translates into a $350,000 value today. Lindbergh had already experienced engine failure twice in 1926, saving his life by parachuting from airplanes to safety, earning him the nickname Lucky. Another pilot had been lost at sea, not able to complete that transatlantic flight.

Lindbergh chose to fly solo in order to use that space and weight for extra fuel needed on the 33 ½ hour flight. It was cold, dark and the sky was full of fog. But he wasn't alone. As he later wrote in his memoir about that long, lonely night.

"Without turning my head, I see them as clearly as though in my normal field of vision. There's no limit to my sight—my skull is one great eye, seeing everywhere at once." He continued, "These phantoms speak with human voices—friendly, vapor-like shapes, without substance, able to vanish or appear at will, to pass in and out through the walls of the fuselage as though no walls were there. Now, many are crowded behind me. Now, only a few remain. First one and then another presses forward to my shoulder to speak above the engine's noise, and then draws back among the group behind. At times, voices come out of the air itself, clear yet far away, traveling through distances that can't be measured by the scale of human miles, familiar voices, conversing and advising on my flight, discussing problems of my navigation, reassuring me, giving me messages of importance unattainable in ordinary life."

In 1916 Ernest Shackleton Antarctic Expedition was stranded when their boat was iced in. His team of three was forced to cross glaciers to a whaling station in Stromness Bay. He reported that he often felt there were four of them, not the three that arrived.

John Geiger has gathered several of these stories and many other accounts, writing their stories in depth in his published book *The Third Man Factor*. He notes, "In every case I found, it was a benevolent helpful companion, not a single example of a malevolent being."

An Angel's Arms

(publ. 2016 A Nosegay of Violets)

My Story

After ten years of an unhappy marriage getting worse, I came up with the idea to flee to Florida taking my four sons with me. They ranged in ages from 5 to 11. My husband Ken's partner in his masonry business lost his family when his wife and children slipped out quietly one day and never came back. It took him a couple years to find her. By then his anger had dissipated and they made sensible arrangements about the children.

After a night of sleeping, actually lying in bed awake, with my youngest son (so Ken wouldn't come after me with his fists) I decided this was the time to go. As soon as he left in the morning, I packed up the kids and Christmas presents and tore out of town. The drive to my mother's house in Ft. Lauderdale, Florida would take approximately 24 hours in these pre-interstate highway days.

In between keeping the kids amused until they fell asleep, thoughts kept running through my mind. What had happened to this marriage that started out so grandly with the big showcase wedding and reception? I had no idea and needed to keep my mind on matters that mattered. Like staying awake after no sleep driving into the second night and how would the kids adjust, how long would it take Ken to come after me and what would he do.

Crossing the Georgia border after midnight reminded me of the swamps on both sides of the two-lane, no-shouldered road. By now it was too dark to see the drop off the road, but I knew those swamps were there. I knew the tops of the telephone poles were even with the roadway. I knew the trees in the swamps were heavily laden with Spanish moss hanging from them like an old man's dirty beard. That was a scary appearance even in broad daylight. At night it conjured up horrible thoughts. I was always terrified of these swamps and practically held my breath all the way through Georgia whenever we drove through here to Mom's for earlier visits. Now was no different. Both hands clutched the steering wheel like our lives depended on it. My knuckles were white with tension.

The adrenaline of fury had worn off hours ago, but the anger was still buried inside me, just below the surface, seething. The desperation for a new life pushed at me. A life of peace and contentment was on order. I was exhausted. The anger had set into my bones after those emotional times and stayed there, building like a concrete wall that wouldn't tumble down.

My thoughts continued to slide through my head, running around and around. They were making me feel worn out. This stretch of road was dark as pitch. My eyes were straining to stay open. No cars had passed by for hours. I kept the radio low, with music trying to stay alert. There weren't any motels on this long stretch of road. There was no place to pull over for even a brief rest. My mind was racing, but my body was dead tired. This was my second night without sleep.

My eyes drooped. The lines in the road were mesmerizing, one after another after another. It was like a thump, thump, thump. Rhythmic. I wished there was a place to pull off the road. There wasn't even a shoulder. I must get the kids to Mom's safely. Maybe opening the window would help. I changed the radio station for livelier music, neither helped. Exhaustion soaked my body through to the bone. My head drooped and my eyes closed.

I jerked up! In front of my car, now pointing over the edge of the drop-off to the swamp was a translucent, bright golden-white glow emanating from a figure whose outline of arms were spread wide surrounding the front of the car! I could see an outline of head, shoulders, arms, and wings. I gasped! She's saved us from going over into the swamp! The swamp that so terrified me, filled with snakes, alligators, and other horrors!

She had stopped us from a certain horrible death! In shock I looked, not being able to say a word or move. I felt, rather than saw, a smile, passive, waiting.

I snapped to attention and turned my head to look over my shoulder. I put the car into reverse and backed slowly onto the macadam. When I looked forward again she was gone.

I was wide awake then, in the still inky night, I quietly drove to the next town, a small one. I pulled into the parking area of a gas station and slept till the first light of dawn.

My first waking moments were thoughts of the *angel.* The possibility that I nearly killed my children lay like an iron weight on my chest. Remorse and comfort chased each other around in my head. It was a night full of more terror than any my husband ever dumped on me. Yet an angel thought us worth saving.

I kept this moment of to myself, never told anyone about it until 2016 when I wrote my tell-all book, *A Nosegay of Violets, A writer's memoir of psychic awakening.* How could I say anything? Who would believe me back in '69?

Since then I've experienced other *moments* but for this book, this was the most important one.

I've also forgiven my husband. He was just being who he was. I've also forgiven myself for the tough decisions I've made that didn't turn out the way I planned.

Chapter Seven

reincarnation & memory

Children are natural teachers when it comes to reincarnation. Often when a soul reincarnates soon after passing over (measuring in time as we know it) they will have full recollection of their earlier life. They freely speak of it until they get hushed up and told to stop talking by their parents or family members who have not opened their minds to the concept, and sometimes when they do. Even without pressure to *be quiet,* children's memories of an earlier incarnation usually begin to fade away by the time they reach five years of age.

Many cases of reincarnation have been documented and proven beyond any doubt at all. There are many books available with documented and fascinating stories about reincarnation.

Sometimes babies are born with physical marks such as scars and birthmarks that were carried from an earlier lifetime. Other times those marks do not show on your body until later in life. Past-Life Regression may give a clear explanation to what happened in that earlier lifetime to leave the marks you now see. You usually carry your likes, dislikes, passions, and interests from one life to the next.

Is It In the Genes?

We were sitting at the table sharing a pot of real ginger-lemon tea. Sweet petit fours and mini éclairs go so well with tea and the stories that come, too. We began discussing uncommon moments that happen.

LaVerne started by saying, "When my granddaughter was a toddler, sitting in a shopping cart in a store, she saw a lady and said, "Hi!"

The lady replied with a, "Hi."

"I've seen you before," said the granddaughter.

"When was that?" Came the question with an amused, curious look.

"When I was driving my car last week." She said in all serious recollection and was about to continue the conversation when her embarrassed mother, who was used to her daughter's comments, started pushing the cart, hurrying to get out of the store before her daughter could say anymore.

Of course young children have no sense of time and she was not making up a story out of the blue. This was clearly an example of reincarnation."

Across Time and Death

A synopsis of a book read that added to my education: Jenny's story began before she was four years old with dreams of Mary dying much too soon in 1932 and leaving her young children motherless. Through her dream as she grew up in England, she came to know Mary's Irish family before Mary died. She saw the cottage they lived in and the life they led. Even daylight brought no relief as she recalled memories of Mary and her children.

Jenny was able to draw a map of how the cottage sat compared to the road next to it. The map became very important. As a young married woman with children, she bought maps trying to locate where Mary's family lived. Finally a new bookstore in town ordered a particular map showing her hand-drawn sketch matched perfectly. She found Malahide, just north of Dublin was where Mary and the children lived!

Jenny and her husband had little money to spare, but she continued her search for her (Mary's) children. By now she knew she was reincarnated from an earlier life which she lived as Mary. She had no idea what she would do when she found her children. And she did find them after 37 years of first coming to know them, searching for them, writing letters, and keeping a journal.

Her main concern was the children, just as Mary was worried about what would happen to them as she lay dying. Sonny, being the oldest had to remain to care for his father. He suffered the beatings his mother endured until he escaped at 17 to join the RAF.

The children were split up. The girls were sent to a convent, except for the baby who was taken by her paternal uncle and adopted. Sonny was not invited to visit so he lost contact. The boys were sent to the Christian Brothers School which they ran away from a year later. Sonny lost contact with them for 50 years. He visited his sisters when he could. After Sonny left, Mary was taken out of the convent and sent home to take care of her father. She escaped as soon as she could and ran away. The father remarried by 1940 and left.

In 1990 Jenny found Jeffrey, the second oldest boy of Mary's eight children. She did her best to explain her thoughts of her being reincarnated, to this man who was old enough to be her father, that in actuality, he was her son! She continued to contact all the children that were still living.

They shared stories with Jenny hearing that Mary's husband John Sutton had been a violent man the same as Jenny's father.

The Sutton children and their offspring asked Jenny and her present day family to stay in touch with her family of a lifetime earlier.

Jenny's complete story can be found in *Across Time and Death, a mother's search for her past life children* by Jenny Cockell. The remaining five children and Jenny gathered together for a documentary made in 1993 in Ireland.

Someone Else's Yesterday

I attended a Past-Life Regression Workshop at the A.R.E. in Virginia Beach (VA) a few years ago where Jeffrey J. Keene spoke about his experiences which he has published in his book *Someone Else's Yesterday.*

His story provides a strong case for belief in reincarnation.

While he and his wife Anna were on a rambling trip from Connecticut looking for antiques, a stop in Sharpsburg, Maryland was the beginning of turning his life completely around. He'd never had any particular interest in the Civil War but while there he had a strong pull to visit the nearby battleground of Antietam. Anna sat in the car while Jeffrey wandered alone onto the battlefield.

I quote: "A wave of grief, sadness, and anger washed over me. Without warning I was suddenly being consumed by burning sensations. Burning tears ran down my cheeks. It became difficult to breathe…."

Getting back to the car wasn't easy because he was so weak.

I believe he stepped into a past time zone into the 19th century life of Brigadier General John B. Gordon of the Sixth Alabama, Confederate States of America. It stirred his curiosity. His search for truth began.

His was a journey of greatly expanding knowledge, history, and comparisons. Jeffrey and Gordon's photos could be interchanged allowing for time differences of clothing. Jeffrey was a Fire Chief in the 90s when he was seeking information about Gordon. He had markings on his body where Gordon had gunshot scars. There were statues, monuments and a gravesite in Georgia discovered and visited, He met Gordon's 80 year old granddaughter. And there is so much more. I highly recommend reading his book.

Stepping into the Past From the Author's Collection

The Hessian

I attended a workshop in 2017 on past-life regression with Joanne DiMaggio MA, CHt at the A.R.E. in Virginia Beach, Virginia. I had been regressed before receiving the same vision as my Reiki healer and once before at the A.R.E. that took me to the *Impressionist* group artists in France's mid-nineteenth century. I put nineteenth century England in my mind because I wanted to explore deeper into that particular area after being familiar with areas when I visited. Instead my lie in France appeared.

My mind was filled with thinking perhaps that day would provide some clues to my *self.* I've often wondered why I preferred *Lincoln Logs* to my brother's *Erector Set;* why I was the only person I knew who didn't bother to watch the landing on the moon. Ho-hum. I've never seen a *Star Wars* movie or anything that resembled it. I love history and the past. I love old houses that pre-date the twentieth century.

In grammar school my nose went up in the air to *Cherry Ames, Nurse of Everything* as I went for the *Nancy Drew* and *Hardy Boys* series that were all about secrets and helping the government fight foreigners during WWII years. Any story about pioneers or the settlers of our country in the early days got my attention.

As an adult I delighted in visiting Mt. Vernon, Monticello, and the Hermitage turning down a day at the beach. Why?

I grew to love Bordentown, where I moved after ending my 15 year marriage. Its history, its houses and its people had a tight hold on me. I never wanted to leave it. Why?

There were approximately 40 of us in the audience. Ms. DiMaggio talked to us about past life regressions using personal stories that enticed us. She led us with instructions as we went into meditation, to time travel for some or for others to drop into a past life. I entered into one of my past lives, not to mid-nineteenth century, but to a place that I surprisingly knew well in this life time. I later described it as putting my foot onto a movie set that was familiar to me. This is how my session evolved.

I stepped onto the path that led to a small wooden bridge, crossed over the stream and found myself on the dirt road that ran through the center of Bordentown, New Jersey. It was an early summer day with puffy white clouds hanging under a clear blue sky. Birds twittered in the tree branches singing to match my cheerful mood as I practically skipped along.

My day gown, known as an undress of cotton was a light cinnamon in color that I wore over my white petticoat. It fell to my ankles. A white ruffle edged my sleeves covering my elbows and matched the little edging of ruffle at my bodice and my mobcap. My clean apron covered the front of my gown. My father had made the leather shoes for my recent seventeenth birthday. They were now covered with dust as the road led me into the business part of town. It was 1777.

Excitement rumbled within me as I had a special assignment today, carrying messages in my basket that circled over my arm, to and from the shoppe keepers right under the noses of the British and Hessians that occupied and strode throughout my town. They were not wanted here.

The British knew we were an important crossroads on the Delaware River with Trenton directly north, Philadelphia to our south and New York to our northeast. Princeton was a short ride away. The Patriots were scattered in the outskirts, sniping musket shots at the enemy to keep them jittery before and after the skirmish had taken place here. They moved their location often so the Brits could not catch them.

None of the Redcoats had never paid any attention to me until today as I was coming out of the butcher's shoppe and crossing the dirt road heading for the baker. I was challenged by a British soldier in his bright red jacket and white pants tucked into high black boots. I cared not to speak to any British if I could help it.

Many of the hired Hessian brutes had been looting and destroying homes looking for items to steal though they were ordered not to. They used the lack of the English language as an excuse of not understanding. At least that's what an officer told my father.

As I reached into my basket to tuck the cloth in tighter a Hessian charged at me with his bayonet stabbing me just below my left breast! I noticed the horrified expressions on the British soldiers standing in the road.

Shocked, my basket seemed to slowly fall to the dirt and I fell with it. Silence. There was dead silence as if the world had ceased all sounds. I took note that the birds stopped their twitter. So slowly I fell, yet my blood spilled out in a rush taking my life with it. I died on the spot.

My spirit rose up from my body and watched from above as the British soldiers gathered around me, the baker who had come out to meet me, slipped unnoticed, picked up my basket with the messages hidden away and quietly went back inside his shop. He knew I was getting whatever help was available and no soldier needed to see what was in that basket!

~

Moving Forward:
In the following information you'll find much that reflects and connects to my past life.

I left my husband and planned to move approximately 10 miles away to Bordentown. I needed a house to live in. I had no money but I did have four sons, ages 14, 12, 10, 8, and a widowed mother to care for. At that time (early '70s) and in that town no one would rent an apartment to a woman without a husband and with four boys. So my brother Bob stepped in to help me.

He took me house shopping. The first house was next to an old firehouse, dark and dilapidated. The second house was outside Bordentown. I insisted that I needed to live in Bordentown, nowhere else. I was adamant especially for a woman with no money. The third house was on the edge of town, across from a small forest and a creek. Perfect.

It was an old house with tan colored faux brick. I didn't mind that, we would be living inside not outside. The Realtor who came took us from the small entry porch, through the front door, into a living room, down a step to a dining room down another step to a large kitchen with an archway opening to a breakfast alcove with wrap around windows. The sun was streaming through them like a new day of promise. I fell in love instantly as my heart fluttered and warmed with a joyful emotion. I turned to the realtor.

"This is home! I'll take it!"

She laughed and said, "You haven't seen the upstairs yet!"

I didn't have to, but I looked at the two bedrooms on the second floor and a bedroom on the third floor. I filled with even more excitement. The old house had steps up and steps down to enter different rooms which were a charming touch to me. I lived there happily for ten years until my boys were young men going their own way. That is not to say I didn't have problems to overcome, I did. But this was home to me and I loved my life there. Bordentown was the place I wanted to be most in the world.

~

Time Moves on:

Peace eventually returned to the Colonies now called the United States of America, and Farnsworth Landing, the original name for the town, was now called Bordentown. Years after the War ended, the same Hessian who ran me through in a haste of anger that he carried with him all his days since early childhood, returned to Bordentown.

He had witnessed an outpouring of love by the residents for me in my brutal death and for each other in defending their homes. He remembered the scene and the emotion that he had never witnessed in his own hometown in Hesse-Cassel Germany. There was no home for him to return. He wanted to become a part of this place if he could hide his heritage from those who still lived there.

More than 200 years later his spirit showed itself in the house built on land he once camped on. That was my home in the mid-70s. I never saw his spirit but a family who lived in my house 30 years after I left it, did. (See *Living with Ghosts* for the full story)

When I sold my house in '82 the couple who bought it for an investment did major remodeling. Nothing wakes spirits in a house more than boarding up windows and moving doorways, etc.

The 17 year old girl in the family told me, "I often felt him watching me. I slept with lights strung around my bedroom to keep the darkness and him at bay."

She slept facing the doorway.

"He never hurt me but seemed fascinated with every move I made. I saw the tall figure outlined with a greatcoat and tall funny-looking hat." (A military hat of the Rev War days.)

"I was unnerved and jittery and refused to stay in the house unless someone else was at home." She said. "The rest of my family had other 'incidents' in the house, but I was the only one to see the military man (Hessian)."

There is no doubt in my mind the spirit in that house was the Hessian soldier who ran me through with his bayonet 200 years prior. I have a jagged birthmark under my left breast that showed itself in my later years. My heart lies behind it.

~

The Town:

At the encouragement of my fiancé, I sold the house and bought a 3-story Victorian apartment house (he later became a partner) which was actually two side-by-side apartment houses joined by a center flight of stairs. I eventually opened a used and rare book shop on the street level. Of course we lived there too, in an 8 room apartment on three levels behind the book shop. I still never wanted to live anywhere else.

The building stood on Farnsworth Avenue which was the main street that ran through the center of town and it was a block down from the core center. The avenue was lined with small, individual shops, taverns, restaurants, two banks, two churches, and the town hall. Beautiful old trees shaded the avenue creating a natural tunnel in some areas. It was the grown up town of where I was bayoneted in the mid-1700s. By this time I had a bit of knowledge about reincarnation but had no solid ideas of a strong connection to me.

The town had been floundering, in the bottom of a cycle, but as the shops began to fill with new owners fulfilling their dreams we began to bring life back into Bordentown. To raise funds for promoting our business district, we held Wine & Cheese affairs in the garden of Mickey and Patti DeSantis.

We business owners, dressed in authentic attire "became" past-Colonial residents who lived in town during the Revolutionary War period. Many were important personages.

I portrayed Patience Lovell Wright, Quaker, dressed all in white as was her way. She was the first American sculptor (wax was her medium) and spied for the Colonies at the court of King George and Queen Charlotte of England during the War years.

She tucked her important findings into the sculptures and sent them to Benjamin Franklin. (I had tucked my information in my basket.) As an avid reader since elementary school I adored stories of passing secret messages and doing my part against the enemy.

~

The 1990s

The British came to town again, bringing Hessians and Native American scouts with them to re-enact skirmishes of the Rev War, This time they were welcomed. Many drifted in and out of my bookshop, lounging in front of the fireplace to chat and nibble on trays of cookies and discuss our town history. So I became a shop owner like the ones I visited in 1777.

I donned my mobcap and my cinnamon colored cotton gown with the white ruffle at the elbows and hem. I put the white apron on but confess I had no leather shoes made by my father. I also *had no idea* that I wore a similar outfit in 1777!

On Sunday morning I went to the booth set up in the Divine Word Seminary field where the soldiers were bivouacked. I sold coffee and donuts to men in British and Patriot uniforms and to the women in suttler's clothes on this last day of their presence in town. (It was another fund raiser.)

At the time I had no idea of a past life experience. I did know happiness overflowed. My smiles burst with each soldier I met, feeling like it was second nature to be in the middle of all these enemies of liberty and freedom from the King and the Patriots that defeated them!

When the British left for the second time, I began writing books that covered the history of this town that was so engrained in me. After 30 years of calling Bordentown my home, of traveling from Australia, to Mexico and the Caribbean, to Africa and Western Europe, I was still content to call this home.

We had two Signers of the Declaration of Independence, Francis Hopkinson and Richard Stockton. Thomas Paine, Father of the American Revolution bought property in Bordentown, never anywhere else. (There is a life size statue of him in town, 1 of 3 world-wide.) I became a founding member of the Thomas Paine Society of Bordentown. Joseph Bonaparte, brother of Napoleon Bonaparte lived here for 20 years. The history goes on. I had lots to write about and still had no idea of my past life here. I did know that it was the happiest years of my life up to that point.

I was fully immersed in the continued development of our business section and constantly worked to make the town better. I was on the committee for the Annual Cranberry Festival and the Iris Festival, the Garden Tour, the Historic Society, the Veterans Memorial and Annual Ball, and Santa sat by my book shop fireside while folks waited for the horse and carriage rides in

December. It's no wonder I worked so hard for this town's improvement. I believed in it and gave my life to keep it free from the British it in 1777.

For my business group, I produced the Annual Walking Tours of Haunted Houses, wrote books about places in town where the spirits (ghosts) were so content that they didn't want to leave either. They wanted to stay. And they did. On the opposite side of town a house had Rev War uniformed soldiers walking through it, making plans. I'd also had experiences with spirits to share and to comfort those who carried fear of the afterlife.

After all, I had shed my blood here and it soaked deep into the dusty road and lay there until I could make Bordentown my home again.

~

The Colonial history of our country was part of me, the people were real. I felt Martha Washington's dismay at her husband being absent from home so much and I *saw* George dying in his bed when I visited Mt. Vernon. As I roamed around Monticello allowing the energy of *all* the inhabitants of the plantation soak into my skin, it became part of my essence.

I ate and drank from pewter mugs at City Tavern in Philadelphia where our Founding Fathers argued and made their plans. I saw the crack in the Liberty Bell and walked through Betsy Ross's tiny house.

As a teenager I ice skated on Princeton's lake where a bonfire warmed our bones and I swam where

Washington crossed the Delaware River on Christmas Eve to turn the tide of the war. We picnicked in that park and climbed Bowmen's Tower where he could see Trenton that fateful night. I learned about 'sleep tight' military beds at the Rev War Barracks in Trenton where our brave men slept.

I grew up saturating myself in Colonial history not realizing I once lived it, that the early American years were dear to me because they were home to me. I was comfortable absorbing all that I learned completely unaware that I was actually revisiting a past life.

Chapter Eight

visits in the night

Visits During the Wee Hours

When we come to understand, interpret, and heed our dreams, we add another tool to our toolbox of clues in finding out who we are, what our purpose is, and what direction is the best path for us. Messengers and Spirit Guides tend to use dreams to place seeds of thought in our subconscious during the night.

If we've asked for guidance or help with our questions in the daylight, answers will come to us during those wee hours of dreamtime. All you have to do before going to sleep is ask, be aware the next few days, pay attention, and act on your answers.

Even when you don't ask, you may receive messages, often from loved ones who have passed on. They, who see all and know all from the other side, will also send us warnings so we can avoid disaster ahead or maybe alerting us to a different path laid out for us.

The key word here is aware. It is your job to take notice, to wake up when you are receiving information from beyond the veil. Keep a notepad and pen beside your bed to jot down these dreams immediately. Key words are often enough to help you recall the dream in the morning. If you lay back down with the idea of recording them in the morning, they will dissolve and you will not be able to recall these often important messages for you.

Recurring dreams have pressing messages for you. Since I was in my 30s I've had dreams of remodeling my first house where I spent 14 years in an unhappy marriage. The dreams were always remodeling that house in all kinds of different plans; a ramp to the front door, the front of the house altered, a back porch added, a kitchen enlarged, a bedroom changed completely, walls torn down, the entire front of the house missing, etc.

Eventually I learned with this particular dream some major change was coming in my life. The dream put me on alert to expect a life-transition, so the interruption in my daily life would not be traumatic, it would not become so unexpected at all.

It took a while for me to piece it all together, but I caught on. It has always been the same house although I've lived in several different houses since then. Only my last dream in 2015 was different. The remodeling was being done in the last house I lived in.

After that first message, which changed my life, moved out of the house, and found some peace in daily living, change continued to be welcome. I like change. It keeps me from becoming stagnant. That does not mean it is easy. Change can be difficult but if that's the message, it will be better for you even if you can't see it at the time.

Recurring dreams are often explained as being connected to fear or unresolved emotional problems. It's the emotion causing the dream to come to you – with answers if you are paying attention. It also allows you to become the observer rather than the one in the middle of the action. This observation shift allows you to be a witness to the issue rather than having the emotion running your life in daylight. Someone is telling you to pay attention! Fix this problem that bothers you, the one that you are not facing.

Dreams are sometimes straightforward but usually not. There is a lot of symbolism that needs interpretation. I use the online Dream Moods and their Dream Dictionary to help untangle some of my convoluted dreams. They cannot give you exact interpretations to your particular scenario but you can use their information as guidelines to mix with your own knowledge to come to a solution. Find the message. Line your spirit and body together as one.

Visitors in the night are different from dream messengers. They are actual spirits that come to you and visit directly. It may sometimes seem like a dream, but it is not something coming from within you. These visitors often are people who have recently passed away. They can also be time travelers passing through, or souls/spirits who are connected to you, and they could be spirits who have not settled on the other side.

Mothers, fathers, and/or other loved ones stop in to remind you that you are loved and they are there to help if you need it. Keep in mind that a person who was lovely in life is certainly not going to harm you.

Pets, especially those that have climbed into bed with you before they passed over are just giving you the comfort they always gave. It is often a pet when you feel movement in your bed but see no one. It is the spirit of your lost pet. Horses have been known to shake a bed or two even if they never climbed into bed in physical form.

Writing a Prayer of Protection that suits you is a good idea for protecting your sleep from unwanted visitors. Below is a prayer that is commonly used. You may substitute any deity name you are most comfortable with.

The Light of God surrounds me,
The Love of God enfolds me,
The Power of God protects me,
The Presence of God watches over me,
And, wherever I am, God is.
Author unknown

A Nighttime Visit

"Even though I didn't socialize with my son's father, he did spend time with his son and my daughter, too. When my son was in college and my daughter at the age where she had gotten her own apartment. A strange thing happened. I was at home on a weekend night while still living in Baltimore. I was just settling into bed when I saw this 6'6" obese man standing next to my bed, urinating!

It took a second or two but then I then realized it was his spirit! His mom called me at 2 a.m. and said, "Bobby died tonight. It was a heart attack."

Probably his size had something to do with that. I thought. I wasn't sure just what happened or why he showed himself to me.

When I paid my respectful visit to her the next day, she asked me outright. "Who told you Bobby died?"

"You did." I said. She looked at me a bit odd. I could see that she had not called me after all.

Later I checked with a close friend of mine who is a psychic. She explained his urinating. It was most likely that he was releasing himself from me.

"In the last five years, I've also experienced someone attempting to lie down in bed next to me. I've felt the bed alter as if it were a physical body climbing into bed. I didn't 'see' anything, just feeling that shift in the bed. It's weird! Twice it happened at home and once at my girlfriend's in Baltimore.

I just said, firmly, "Out! You're not wanted here!" I need to find out more on this happening, see if I can learn to understand it.

Dreams can be puzzling. One night I dreamed that I was making particular sandwiches for lunch. I forgot the dream as soon as I woke up. That very day when I started to make a particular sandwich, for lunch, it hit me that I had dreamed this exactly as I was now doing. *STOP!* I said to myself. This is a bit crazy. Yet, it is what it is. (precognitive dreaming) It's happened before, but I don't write these things down, so the memory of them fades away."

Nocturnal Visits

When I was writing *Major Fraser's, A History of a House,* I wrote more about Major Thomas Fraser than anyone else who lived in or owned the house, dating back to the 1700s. The research stayed with me and hung around the back of my mind awake or not. Soon after the writing was finished, visitors woke me up at the usual wee hour of the morning. (Always around 3 a.m. give or take some.) The Major's wife, nee Anne Loughton Smith came to me, said she wanted me to tell her story, too. She also told me exactly where to find the info I needed for her background! (Think about researching accurate information in the 1700s for a Smith.)

Like children that are alive today, *their* children came to me, yanking my chain, wanting me to write their stories, too! They also lived extraordinary lives including daughter Caroline Georgina who married the nephew of Napoleon Bonaparte. He was a prince, so Caroline Georgina became a princess. She lived in poverty until she followed her husband to France and lived a royal life. It took some time before I went back to getting a good night's sleep!

The *ghost children* who live in Alice and Duane's house in Warren Plains (where I attended a Tea Party with them (see Ghostly Spirits of Warren County &

Beyond) asked permission to come *visit* me one night. How could I refuse after they invited me into their home, for Tea? Annie and Lauren and friends were very polite and giggly when they came (at that 3 a.m. hour again) and honored it when I restricted their *visit* to one time only. I really do need my night time sleep. Before their visit I had not known their names.

About the Author

When I was five years old Virus Pneumonia held me between life and death for a couple days. I stayed in St. Francis Hospital's Children's Ward for a week. Mom told me that a 'new' drug called Penicillin brought me back to life and good health again. I only remember the recovery, the attention and teddy bears given to me to hug.

I don't know if the state of the illness had anything to do with my development of psychic ability or not. My mother's mother Elizabeth was fully developed. My eldest brother Albert was somewhat developed. My mother, only as far as her children were concerned.

I always had a *sense* about people. Even very young there were people I stayed away from, out of their range where they could harm me. I *knew* when to cross the street to create a distance. I thought everyone had that ability. I spent a lot of alone time roaming and exploring on my bike while growing up.

I continued that habit even after another girl moved into the neighborhood when I was about nine. By the time I was ten I was moving into responsible years, babysitting to earn money. I didn't roam on my bike much after that.

My earliest recollection of anything out of the ordinary happening to me was when I was in my late teens I *saw* a boy on a bicycle run into my car a few minutes before it actually happened. Around this time I also began hearing my name being called when I could see no one. I was married by then.

Albert, my oldest brother moved to Puerto Rico. These were the days when telephoning was so expensive that it halted conversation flow. So he and I wrote letters to stay in touch. He never made major changes without consulting a Tarot Card reader. He reluctantly told me about some of his psychic experiences. Fortunately I could write to him to discuss moments that happened to me. He told me to keep it to myself and not to talk about it to anyone.

Reading was my answer. Always, reading and work were my 'go to' to get through any unhappiness, stress, or problems I had no ideas how to solve. Also I read to learn about life and what I needed to know. I didn't have easy access to books, so I was limited to my choices. I did join a book club and received a book each month. In those days Readers' Digest Condensed Books were popular and a good source for my thirst.

It was several years later but the first books I read on death, dying and the afterlife were:

Raymond Moody	Life After Life:
Brian L. Weiss	Many Lives, Many Masters:
Thomas Sugrue	There is a River (Edgar Cayce)
Jess Stearn	Edgar Cayce, Sleeping Prophet

72706885R00133

Made in the USA
Columbia, SC
02 September 2019

Origins of the Dandie Dinmont Terrier

History of the Breed

Characteristics of the Dandie Dinmont Terrier

Physical Appearance of the Dandie Dinmont Terrier

Temperament of the Dandie Dinmont Terrier

Personality of the Dandie Dinmont Terrier

Bond between the Dandie Dinmont Terrier and its Owner

Training a Dandie Dinmont Terrier

Socializing a Dandie Dinmont Terrier

Exercising a Dandie Dinmont Terrier

Feeding a Dandie Dinmont Terrier

Grooming a Dandie Dinmont Terrier

Health Concerns of the Dandie Dinmont Terrier

Preventative Care for the Dandie Dinmont Terrier

Regular Check-Ups for the Dandie Dinmont Terrier

Dandie Dinmont Terrier Puppyhood

Adolescent Years of a Dandie Dinmont Terrier

Adult Life of a Dandie Dinmont Terrier

Senior Years of a Dandie Dinmont Terrier

Breeding Dandie Dinmont Terriers

Pregnancy and Birth in Dandie Dinmont Terriers

Raising Dandie Dinmont Terrier Puppies

Socializing Dandie Dinmont Terrier Puppies

Health Concerns for Dandie Dinmont Terrier Puppies

Training Dandie Dinmont Terrier Puppies

Competitions for Dandie Dinmont Terriers

Therapy and Service Work for Dandie Dinmont Terriers

Hunting Background of Dandie Dinmont Terriers

Fun Activities for Dandie Dinmont Terriers

Traveling with Dandie Dinmont Terriers

Living in Different Environments with Dandie Dinmont Terriers

Living with Children and Dandie Dinmont Terriers

Origins of the Dandie Dinmont Terrier

The origins of the Dandie Dinmont Terrier can be traced back to the Scottish Borders, where they were originally bred to hunt otters and badgers. The breed is named after a character in Sir Walter Scott's novel "Guy Mannering," in which a farmer named Dandie Dinmont owned several terriers. The breed is believed to have been developed in the 18th century by crossing several different terrier breeds, including the Bedlington Terrier and the Skye Terrier. Over time, the Dandie Dinmont Terrier became recognized as a distinct breed, and today they are cherished for their unique appearance and lively personality.

History of the Breed

The Dandie Dinmont Terrier has a rich history dating back to the 1700s. The breed was developed in the Scottish Borders, where they were used to hunt otters and badgers, which were considered pests by farmers. The breed was named after a character in Sir Walter Scott's novel "Guy Mannering," in which a farmer named Dandie Dinmont owned several terriers.

In the early 1800s, the breed became popular with British nobility and was exhibited at dog shows. In 1875, the Dandie Dinmont Terrier Club was formed in the UK, and the breed was officially recognized by the Kennel Club in 1876.

The breed's popularity declined after World War II, but thanks to the efforts of dedicated breeders, the Dandie Dinmont Terrier has survived and even thrived in recent years. Today, the breed is still used for hunting, but is also valued as a companion and family pet.

Characteristics of the Dandie Dinmont Terrier

The Dandie Dinmont Terrier is a small, sturdy breed with several unique physical and personality traits. Here are some of the key characteristics of the breed:

1. *Size: The Dandie Dinmont Terrier is a small breed, typically weighing between 18 and 24 pounds and standing 8-11 inches tall at the shoulder.*

2. *Coat: The breed's coat is unique, with a combination of a soft undercoat and a wiry outer coat that gives them a distinctive appearance. The coat colors can be pepper (grey) or mustard (brown).*

3. *Personality: Dandie Dinmont Terriers are known for their lively and affectionate personalities. They are highly intelligent and can be trained to perform a variety of tasks.*

4. *Energy Level: Despite their small size, Dandie Dinmont Terriers are quite active and require regular exercise to stay healthy and happy.*

5. *Loyalty: Dandie Dinmont Terriers are fiercely loyal to their owners and make great companions for families and individuals alike.*

6. *Protective: The breed can be protective of their owners and territory, making them good watchdogs.*

7. *Health: Like all breeds, the Dandie Dinmont Terrier can be prone to certain health issues, such as hip dysplasia and back problems. It's important to work with a reputable breeder and monitor your dog's health closely.*

Physical Appearance of the Dandie Dinmont Terrier

The Dandie Dinmont Terrier is a small breed with a distinctive appearance. Here are some key physical traits of the breed:

1. Size: The Dandie Dinmont Terrier is a small breed, typically weighing between 18 and 24 pounds and standing 8-11 inches tall at the shoulder.

2. Coat: The breed's coat is unique, with a combination of a soft undercoat and a wiry outer coat that gives them a distinctive appearance. The coat colors can be pepper (grey) or mustard (brown).

3. Head: The Dandie Dinmont Terrier has a large, broad head with a distinctive topknot of hair on the crown.

4. Eyes: The breed has large, round, dark brown eyes that are set wide apart.

5. Ears: The Dandie Dinmont Terrier's ears are set low and hang close to the head, with a thin layer of hair covering them.

6. Body: The breed has a long, low-slung body with a deep chest and muscular legs.

7. Tail: The Dandie Dinmont Terrier's tail is short and carried high, often with a slight curve.

Overall, the Dandie Dinmont Terrier has a unique and charming appearance that sets them apart from other breeds. Their distinctive coat and topknot make them instantly recognizable, and their lively personalities make them beloved pets and companions.

Temperament of the Dandie Dinmont Terrier

The Dandie Dinmont Terrier is a breed with a lively, affectionate, and loyal temperament. Here are some key traits of the breed's personality:

1. *Playful: Dandie Dinmont Terriers are known for their playful personalities and love to interact with their owners.*
2. *Affectionate: The breed is highly affectionate and enjoys spending time with their owners. They love to be petted and cuddled and will often seek out attention.*

3. *Loyal: Dandie Dinmont Terriers are fiercely loyal to their owners and will protect their family members if they feel threatened.*

4. *Independent: Despite their affectionate nature, Dandie Dinmont Terriers can be independent and strong-willed. They may need a firm hand in training to prevent them from becoming stubborn.*

5. *Alert: The breed is known for their alertness and make excellent watchdogs. They are quick to bark at any perceived threat to their territory.*

6. *Intelligent: Dandie Dinmont Terriers are intelligent and respond well to training. They excel in obedience and agility competitions.*

7. *Social: The breed generally gets along well with other dogs and can be friendly with strangers if socialized properly.*

Overall, the Dandie Dinmont Terrier has a charming personality that endears them to their owners. They make great companions and can adapt to a variety of lifestyles, from city apartments to rural homes.

Personality of the Dandie Dinmont Terrier

The Dandie Dinmont Terrier is a breed with a unique personality that sets them apart from other terrier breeds. Here are some key personality traits of the Dandie Dinmont Terrier:

1. *Independent: Dandie Dinmont Terriers are known for their independent nature. They have a strong sense of self and can be quite stubborn at times.*
2. *Loyal: The breed is fiercely loyal to their owners and will protect their family members if they feel threatened. They form strong bonds with their owners and enjoy spending time with them.*
3. *Playful: Dandie Dinmont Terriers are known for their playful personalities. They love to play games and interact with their owners.*
4. *Intelligent: The breed is highly intelligent and responds well to training. They excel in obedience and agility competitions.*
5. *Alert: Dandie Dinmont Terriers are alert and make excellent watchdogs. They are quick to bark at any perceived threat to their territory.*
6. *Affectionate: While the breed can be independent, they are also affectionate with their owners. They enjoy being petted and cuddled and will often seek out attention.*
7. *Social: Dandie Dinmont Terriers generally get along well with other dogs and can be friendly with strangers if socialized properly.*

Overall, the Dandie Dinmont Terrier has a unique and charming personality that makes them a beloved breed. They are loyal, intelligent, and playful, and make great companions for families and individuals alike.

Bond between the Dandie Dinmont Terrier and its Owner

The bond between a Dandie Dinmont Terrier and its owner can be quite strong. Here are some reasons why:

1. *Loyalty: Dandie Dinmont Terriers are known for their loyalty to their owners. They form strong bonds with their human family members and will do anything to protect them.*

2. *Affectionate: The breed is also affectionate and loves to spend time with their owners. They enjoy being petted, cuddled, and playing games together.*

3. *Dependability: Owners of Dandie Dinmont Terriers often appreciate their dependability. They can be counted on to be there for their owners and provide emotional support when needed.*

4. *Playfulness: Dandie Dinmont Terriers are a playful breed that loves to engage in activities with their owners, such as going for walks or playing fetch. This shared activity can help to strengthen the bond between the owner and their pet.*

5. Companionship: Dandie Dinmont Terriers make excellent companions and are happy to be by their owner's side. Their presence can provide comfort and support during difficult times.

Overall, the bond between a Dandie Dinmont Terrier and its owner can be quite special. Their loyalty, affection, and dependability make them a beloved companion for many people.

Training a Dandie Dinmont Terrier

Training a Dandie Dinmont Terrier can be a rewarding experience, but it can also require patience and consistency. Here are some tips for training a Dandie Dinmont Terrier:

1. *Start early: It's important to start training your Dandie Dinmont Terrier as early as possible. This can help to establish good habits and prevent bad ones from forming.*

2. *Use positive reinforcement: Dandie Dinmont Terriers respond well to positive reinforcement training. This means rewarding good behavior with treats, praise, or toys.*

3. *Be consistent: Consistency is key when training a Dandie Dinmont Terrier. Use the same commands and training techniques every time to avoid confusion.*

4. *Keep training sessions short: Dandie Dinmont Terriers have short attention spans, so keep training sessions short and focused. Aim for 10-15 minute sessions a few times a day.*

5. *Socialize your Dandie Dinmont Terrier: Socialization is important for any dog, and Dandie Dinmont Terriers are no exception. Introduce them to new people, animals, and environments to help them become well-adjusted and confident.*

6. *Provide mental stimulation: Dandie Dinmont Terriers are intelligent dogs that require mental stimulation. Providing them with puzzle toys or interactive games can help keep them mentally stimulated.*

7. *Stay patient: Training a Dandie Dinmont Terrier can take time, so it's important to stay patient and not get frustrated.*

Remember that consistency and positive reinforcement are key.

Overall, training a Dandie Dinmont Terrier can be a fun and rewarding experience. With patience, consistency, and positive reinforcement, your Dandie Dinmont Terrier can learn to be a well-behaved and well-adjusted companion.

Socializing a Dandie Dinmont Terrier

Socializing a Dandie Dinmont Terrier is an important aspect of their development. Socialization refers to exposing your dog to different people, animals, and environments, and helping them learn how to interact with them in a positive way. Here are some tips for socializing your Dandie Dinmont Terrier:

1. *Start early: Socialization should begin when your Dandie Dinmont Terrier is a puppy. This is when they are most receptive to new experiences and can learn to adapt to them more easily.*

2. *Introduce them to new people: Take your Dandie Dinmont Terrier to different places where they can meet new people. This can include parks, pet stores, and even cafes that allow dogs.*

3. *Expose them to different animals: Introducing your Dandie Dinmont Terrier to other dogs and animals can help them learn to socialize and interact appropriately.*

4. *Practice obedience training: Obedience training can help your Dandie Dinmont Terrier learn how to behave appropriately in social situations. Teach them basic commands such as sit, stay, and come.*

5. *Use positive reinforcement: Reward your Dandie Dinmont Terrier with treats and praise when they exhibit good behavior during socialization.*

6. *Take it slow: Don't overwhelm your Dandie Dinmont Terrier with too many new experiences all at once. Start with one or two new experiences at a time, and gradually introduce them to more.*

7. *Be patient: Socialization is a gradual process, and it may take some time for your Dandie Dinmont Terrier to feel comfortable in new situations. Be patient and allow them to go at their own pace.*

Overall, socializing your Dandie Dinmont Terrier is an important part of their development. It can help them become a well-adjusted and confident companion that is comfortable in a variety of situations.

Exercising a Dandie Dinmont Terrier

Exercising a Dandie Dinmont Terrier is important for their overall health and well-being. These dogs have moderate exercise needs and can adapt to a range of activity levels, but it's important to provide them with enough exercise to keep them healthy and happy. Here are some tips for exercising a Dandie Dinmont Terrier:

1. *Start with short walks: Begin with short walks of 10-15 minutes and gradually increase the duration and intensity of exercise as your Dandie Dinmont Terrier builds endurance.*

2. *Provide mental stimulation: Dandie Dinmont Terriers are intelligent dogs that require mental stimulation to stay happy and healthy. Provide them with toys that challenge their problem-solving abilities, such as puzzle toys or interactive games.*

3. *Consider indoor exercise: Dandie Dinmont Terriers can adapt to indoor exercise such as playing fetch or tug-of-war. This can be a good option if the weather is bad or if you don't have access to outdoor space.*

4. *Incorporate training: Dandie Dinmont Terriers enjoy obedience training and agility, which can provide both physical and mental exercise.*

5. *Go for regular walks: Regular walks are important for Dandie Dinmont Terriers. Aim for at least one 30-45 minute walk per day to keep them healthy and prevent boredom.*

6. *Consider swimming: Swimming can be a great low-impact exercise for Dandie Dinmont Terriers. Make sure to*

supervise your dog closely and provide them with a life jacket if necessary.

7. *Stay mindful of the weather: Dandie Dinmont Terriers are sensitive to extreme temperatures, so make sure to avoid exercising them in extreme heat or cold.*

Overall, Dandie Dinmont Terriers have moderate exercise needs and enjoy a variety of activities. By providing them with enough physical and mental exercise, you can help them stay healthy, happy, and well-adjusted.

Feeding a Dandie Dinmont Terrier

Feeding a Dandie Dinmont Terrier is an important aspect of their care. These dogs have unique nutritional needs that should be met to keep them healthy and happy. Here are some tips for feeding a Dandie Dinmont Terrier:

1. *Choose high-quality dog food: Look for dog food that is specifically formulated for small breed dogs, and choose a high-quality brand that uses wholesome ingredients.*

2. *Feed small, frequent meals: Dandie Dinmont Terriers have small stomachs and may be prone to digestive issues if they eat too much at once. Consider feeding them small, frequent meals throughout the day rather than one or two large meals.*

3. *Monitor portion sizes: Dandie Dinmont Terriers are prone to obesity, so it's important to monitor their portion sizes and avoid overfeeding them. Follow the recommended feeding guidelines on the dog food packaging, and adjust the amount as needed based on your dog's individual needs.*

4. *Provide fresh water: Make sure your Dandie Dinmont Terrier has access to fresh water at all times. Change their water bowl frequently to ensure that the water is clean and fresh.*

5. *Avoid table scraps: While it may be tempting to give your Dandie Dinmont Terrier table scraps or human food, it's best to avoid this. Human food can be high in calories, salt, and fat, which can be harmful to your dog's health.*

6. *Consider a raw diet: Some Dandie Dinmont Terrier owners opt for a raw diet for their dogs. This can provide a variety of health benefits, but it's important to do your research and make sure that you are feeding your dog a balanced and nutritious diet.*

7. *Monitor your dog's weight: Keep an eye on your Dandie Dinmont Terrier's weight and body condition, and adjust their diet as needed to ensure that they are maintaining a healthy weight.*

Overall, feeding a Dandie Dinmont Terrier is an important part of their care. By providing them with a balanced and nutritious diet, you can help keep them healthy and happy for years to come.

Grooming a Dandie Dinmont Terrier

Grooming a Dandie Dinmont Terrier is an important part of their care. These dogs have a unique coat that requires regular maintenance to keep it in good condition. Here are some tips for grooming a Dandie Dinmont Terrier:

1. *Brush regularly: Dandie Dinmont Terriers have a double coat that can become tangled and matted if not brushed regularly. Use a slicker brush to remove any tangles or mats, and then use a comb to smooth out the coat.*

2. *Bathe occasionally: While Dandie Dinmont Terriers do not require frequent baths, they should be bathed occasionally to*

keep their coat clean and free from dirt and debris. Use a mild dog shampoo and rinse thoroughly.

3. *Trim nails: Keep your Dandie Dinmont Terrier's nails trimmed to prevent them from becoming too long and causing discomfort or injury. Use a dog nail trimmer and be careful not to cut the quick, which is a blood vessel that runs through the nail.*

4. *Clean ears: Dandie Dinmont Terriers are prone to ear infections, so it's important to keep their ears clean and free from wax and debris. Use a damp cloth or cotton ball to gently clean the inside of the ear, and avoid using cotton swabs, which can push debris further into the ear.*

5. *Monitor teeth: Like all dogs, Dandie Dinmont Terriers are prone to dental problems. Brush your dog's teeth regularly with a dog toothbrush and toothpaste, and consider providing dental chews or toys to help keep their teeth clean.*

6. *Trim hair around eyes and ears: Dandie Dinmont Terriers have long hair around their eyes and ears that can grow too long and cause discomfort or impede vision. Use scissors to carefully trim the hair around these areas.*

7. *Visit a professional groomer: If you are not comfortable grooming your Dandie Dinmont Terrier yourself, consider taking them to a professional groomer for regular grooming appointments. A groomer can help keep your dog's coat in*

good condition and provide additional grooming services such as trimming the hair around the paw pads and sanitary areas.

Overall, grooming a Dandie Dinmont Terrier requires regular maintenance to keep their unique coat in good condition and to prevent health problems. By following these tips, you can help keep your Dandie Dinmont Terrier looking and feeling their best.

Health Concerns of the Dandie Dinmont Terrier

Like all breeds, Dandie Dinmont Terriers are prone to certain health concerns. Some of the most common health issues that affect this breed include:

1. *Intervertebral Disc Disease (IVDD): This is a condition in which the discs between the vertebrae of the spine degenerate and can lead to pain, weakness, and even paralysis.*

2. *Eye problems: Dandie Dinmont Terriers are prone to several eye conditions, including cataracts, glaucoma, and progressive retinal atrophy (PRA).*

3. *Hypothyroidism: This is a condition in which the thyroid gland does not produce enough hormones, which can lead to weight gain, lethargy, and skin problems.*

4. *Allergies: Dandie Dinmont Terriers can be prone to allergies, which can cause skin irritation, itching, and ear infections.*

5. *Canine Hip Dysplasia: This is a condition in which the hip joint does not develop properly and can lead to pain, lameness, and arthritis.*

6. *Patellar Luxation: This is a condition in which the kneecap moves out of place, which can cause pain and lameness.*

7. *Portosystemic Shunt: This is a congenital condition in which a blood vessel bypasses the liver, which can lead to a buildup of toxins in the bloodstream.*

To help prevent health issues in your Dandie Dinmont Terrier, it's important to feed them a healthy diet, provide regular exercise, and schedule routine veterinary checkups. Early detection and treatment of health issues can also help to prevent more serious problems from developing.

Preventative Care for the Dandie Dinmont Terrier

Preventative care is an important aspect of keeping your Dandie Dinmont Terrier healthy and happy. Here are some preventative care measures to consider for your furry friend:

1. *Regular Veterinary Checkups: Routine checkups with your veterinarian can help catch potential health problems early on, before they become more serious. Your vet can also provide advice on nutrition, exercise, and other aspects of your dog's health.*

2. *Vaccinations: Vaccinations are crucial in preventing infectious diseases in your Dandie Dinmont Terrier. Make sure to keep*

up with their vaccination schedule as recommended by your veterinarian.

3. *Parasite Prevention: Dandie Dinmont Terriers can be prone to parasites such as fleas, ticks, and heartworms. Speak to your veterinarian about the appropriate parasite prevention measures for your dog, such as monthly flea and tick prevention and regular heartworm testing and prevention.*

4. *Dental Care: Regular dental care, such as brushing your dog's teeth and providing dental chews, can help prevent dental disease and keep your Dandie Dinmont Terrier's teeth healthy.*

5. *Exercise: Regular exercise is important for maintaining your Dandie Dinmont Terrier's physical and mental health. Make sure to provide daily exercise appropriate for their age and physical condition.*

6. *Nutrition: Feeding your Dandie Dinmont Terrier a balanced and nutritious diet is essential for their overall health and well-being. Speak to your veterinarian about the appropriate diet for your dog's age and activity level.*

By following these preventative care measures, you can help ensure that your Dandie Dinmont Terrier lives a healthy and happy life.

Regular Check-Ups for the Dandie Dinmont Terrier

Regular check-ups with a veterinarian are important for maintaining the health of your Dandie Dinmont Terrier. During these check-ups, the veterinarian will examine your dog's overall health and check for any signs of illness or disease.

The frequency of check-ups can vary depending on your dog's age, health status, and any medical conditions they may have. As a general rule, it is recommended to schedule a check-up at least once a year for adult dogs, and more frequently for puppies and senior dogs.

During a check-up, the veterinarian will perform a physical exam that may include:

- *Checking your dog's eyes, ears, and nose for signs of infection or abnormalities.*
- *Examining your dog's skin and coat for any signs of irritation, inflammation, or parasites.*
- *Checking your dog's mouth and teeth for dental problems, such as tartar buildup, gum disease, or tooth decay.*
- *Listening to your dog's heart and lungs to detect any abnormal sounds or rhythms.*
- *Palpating your dog's abdomen and lymph nodes to check for any signs of swelling or abnormalities.*

The veterinarian may also recommend additional testing or diagnostic procedures, such as bloodwork or urine analysis, depending on the results of the physical exam or any specific concerns you may have about your dog's health.

Regular check-ups are an important part of preventative care for your Dandie Dinmont Terrier and can help catch potential health problems early on, before they become more serious.

Dandie Dinmont Terrier Puppyhood

Dandie Dinmont Terrier puppies are adorable and playful, but they require special care and attention during their first few months of life. Here are some things to keep in mind during your Dandie Dinmont Terrier puppy's early months:

1. *Socialization: Early socialization is important for puppies to learn appropriate behaviors and how to interact with people and other dogs. Introduce your puppy to a variety of experiences, people, and animals in a positive and safe way.*
2. *Training: Start training your Dandie Dinmont Terrier puppy early on to establish good habits and behaviors. Positive reinforcement techniques, such as treats and praise, can be effective in training your puppy.*
3. *Exercise: Puppies need plenty of exercise and playtime to help them develop physically and mentally. However, make*

sure not to over-exercise your puppy, as their bones and joints are still developing.

4. *Nutrition: Feeding your puppy a high-quality, age-appropriate diet is important for their growth and development. Consult with your veterinarian for recommendations on the best diet for your Dandie Dinmont Terrier puppy.*
5. *Vaccinations: Make sure your puppy is up-to-date on all necessary vaccinations to protect them from common diseases.*
6. *Grooming: Regular grooming is important for your Dandie Dinmont Terrier puppy's coat and skin health. Get them used to regular grooming sessions from an early age to make it easier as they grow older.*
7. *Puppy-proofing: Make sure your home is safe for your puppy by puppy-proofing your living space. This includes removing any hazardous items or substances and securing any loose items that could be a choking hazard.*

By providing proper care and attention during your Dandie Dinmont Terrier puppy's early months, you can help set them up for a healthy and happy life.

Adolescent Years of a Dandie Dinmont Terrier

The adolescent years of a Dandie Dinmont Terrier can be challenging for both the dog and their owner. Here are some things to keep in mind during this stage of their development:

1. *Behavior: Adolescence is a time when dogs may start testing boundaries and exhibiting behaviors that can be frustrating for their owners. It's important to continue with consistent training and positive reinforcement techniques to help your Dandie Dinmont Terrier understand what behaviors are acceptable.*

2. Exercise: Adolescents still need plenty of exercise and playtime to keep them physically and mentally stimulated. Consider increasing their exercise routine, but also be careful not to over-exercise them.

3. Nutrition: It's important to continue feeding your Dandie Dinmont Terrier a high-quality, age-appropriate diet during their adolescent years to support their growth and development.

4. Health: Regular veterinary check-ups are important during adolescence to ensure that your Dandie Dinmont Terrier is growing and developing properly. It's also important to continue with any necessary vaccinations and preventative care.

5. Grooming: Regular grooming is still important during adolescence to maintain your Dandie Dinmont Terrier's coat and skin health.

6. Socialization: Continue to expose your Dandie Dinmont Terrier to a variety of experiences, people, and animals to help them become well-rounded and well-behaved adults.

7. Patience: Adolescent years can be challenging for both dogs and their owners. It's important to have patience and understanding during this stage of their development.

By providing proper care and attention during your Dandie Dinmont Terrier's adolescent years, you can help them grow into a happy and well-behaved adult.

Adult Life of a Dandie Dinmont Terrier

The adult life of a Dandie Dinmont Terrier is characterized by their playful, loyal, and independent nature. Here are some things to keep in mind during this stage of their life:

1. *Exercise: Adult Dandie Dinmont Terriers still need regular exercise and playtime to maintain their physical and mental health. They enjoy going for walks, playing fetch, and exploring new environments.*

2. *Nutrition: A healthy, balanced diet is important to maintain your Dandie Dinmont Terrier's health and well-being throughout their adult years. It's important to feed them a diet that is appropriate for their age, weight, and activity level.*

3. *Grooming: Regular grooming is essential to keep your Dandie Dinmont Terrier's coat and skin healthy and free of matting. They have a unique coat that requires special attention, including regular brushing, trimming, and stripping.*

4. *Health: Regular veterinary check-ups are important to ensure that your Dandie Dinmont Terrier remains healthy and free*

of any medical conditions. It's important to stay up-to-date on vaccinations and preventative care.

5. Training: Although Dandie Dinmont Terriers are intelligent and independent, they still benefit from continued training and socialization throughout their adult years. Consistency, patience, and positive reinforcement are key to successful training.

6. Bonding: Dandie Dinmont Terriers form strong bonds with their owners and enjoy spending time with them. They are affectionate and playful, and they thrive on attention and affection.

By providing your Dandie Dinmont Terrier with proper care, attention, and training during their adult years, you can help them live a happy and healthy life.

Senior Years of a Dandie Dinmont Terrier

The senior years of a Dandie Dinmont Terrier are a time when they may start to slow down and experience some age-related health concerns. Here are some things to keep in mind during this stage of their life:

1. Health: Regular veterinary check-ups become even more important as your Dandie Dinmont Terrier enters their senior years. Age-related health concerns may include arthritis, vision and hearing loss, dental issues, and cognitive decline.

2. *Nutrition: A healthy diet is important to maintain your Dandie Dinmont Terrier's health as they age. Their nutritional needs may change, and it may be necessary to switch to a senior dog food that is formulated to meet their specific needs.*

3. *Exercise: While your senior Dandie Dinmont Terrier may not be as active as they once were, regular exercise is still important to keep them healthy and maintain their mobility. Short, gentle walks or indoor playtime may be more appropriate for their age and energy level.*

4. *Comfort: Older Dandie Dinmont Terriers may have difficulty with stairs or getting in and out of vehicles. Providing comfortable bedding and easy access to food and water can help make their senior years more comfortable.*

5. *Bonding: Senior Dandie Dinmont Terriers still enjoy spending time with their owners and benefit from regular interaction and attention. They may become more affectionate and cuddly as they age.*

By providing your senior Dandie Dinmont Terrier with the proper care and attention, you can help them age gracefully and comfortably. Regular veterinary check-ups, a healthy diet, gentle exercise, and plenty of love and attention can help your senior Dandie Dinmont Terrier live out their golden years in comfort and happiness.

Breeding Dandie Dinmont Terriers

Breeding Dandie Dinmont Terriers should be done responsibly and with the intention of improving the breed. Here are some things to consider if you are interested in breeding Dandie Dinmont Terriers:

1. Health: Before breeding your Dandie Dinmont Terrier, it's important to ensure that they are healthy and free from any genetic health concerns that could be passed on to their offspring. Health testing should be performed by a veterinarian or veterinary geneticist to identify any potential issues.

2. Genetics: Dandie Dinmont Terriers are a relatively rare breed, and breeding should be done with the intention of preserving and improving the breed. It's important to carefully select a breeding pair that complements each other in terms of physical and behavioral characteristics, as well as genetic health.
3. Registration: Dandie Dinmont Terrier breeding should only be done with registered dogs to maintain the integrity of the breed. Breeders should adhere to the breed standard set forth by the American Kennel Club or other recognized breed organizations.
4. Ethics: Responsible breeding means putting the health and well-being of the dogs first. Breeders should ensure that their dogs are well-cared for, and that their puppies go to loving, responsible homes.
5. Education: Breeders should continually educate themselves about the breed, genetics, and best breeding practices. They should also be willing to educate potential puppy owners about the breed and their responsibilities as owners.

Breeding Dandie Dinmont Terriers can be a rewarding experience for those who are committed to improving the breed and ensuring the health and well-being of their dogs and their offspring. However, it is important to approach breeding with care and responsibility to maintain the integrity of the breed and promote the health and happiness of the dogs involved.

Breeding Dandie Dinmont Terriers should be done responsibly and with the intention of improving the breed. Here are some things to consider if you are interested in breeding Dandie Dinmont Terriers:

1. *Health: Before breeding your Dandie Dinmont Terrier, it's important to ensure that they are healthy and free from any genetic health concerns that could be passed on to their offspring. Health testing should be performed by a veterinarian or veterinary geneticist to identify any potential issues.*

2. *Genetics: Dandie Dinmont Terriers are a relatively rare breed, and breeding should be done with the intention of preserving and improving the breed. It's important to carefully select a breeding pair that complements each other in terms of physical and behavioral characteristics, as well as genetic health.*

3. *Registration: Dandie Dinmont Terrier breeding should only be done with registered dogs to maintain the integrity of the breed. Breeders should adhere to the breed standard set forth by the American Kennel Club or other recognized breed organizations.*

4. *Ethics: Responsible breeding means putting the health and well-being of the dogs first. Breeders should ensure that their*

dogs are well-cared for, and that their puppies go to loving, responsible homes.

5. *Education: Breeders should continually educate themselves about the breed, genetics, and best breeding practices. They should also be willing to educate potential puppy owners about the breed and their responsibilities as owners.*

Breeding Dandie Dinmont Terriers can be a rewarding experience for those who are committed to improving the breed and ensuring the health and well-being of their dogs and their offspring. However, it is important to approach breeding with care and responsibility to maintain the integrity of the breed and promote the health and happiness of the dogs involved.

Pregnancy and Birth in Dandie Dinmont Terriers

Pregnancy and birth in Dandie Dinmont Terriers, as with any breed, should be carefully monitored and managed to ensure the health of the mother and her puppies. Here are some things to consider:

1. *Pregnancy: The gestation period for Dandie Dinmont Terriers is approximately 63 days. During pregnancy, the mother should be given a nutritious diet and regular veterinary check-ups to ensure that both she and her puppies are healthy. It's important to avoid exposing the mother to any potential hazards, such as toxins, parasites, or other animals that could transmit diseases.*

2. Preparing for birth: As the due date approaches, the mother should be given a comfortable and safe place to give birth, such as a whelping box. It's important to have all necessary supplies on hand, such as clean towels, scissors, and sterile instruments. It's also a good idea to have a plan in place for emergency situations.

3. Labor and delivery: Dandie Dinmont Terriers typically have small litters, with an average of 3-4 puppies. During labor and delivery, it's important to monitor the mother and her puppies closely for any signs of distress or complications. In some cases, intervention may be necessary, such as helping with the delivery of a stuck puppy or providing oxygen to a struggling puppy.

4. Post-birth care: After the puppies are born, it's important to monitor them closely to ensure that they are nursing properly and gaining weight. The mother should continue to receive a nutritious diet and regular veterinary check-ups. It's also important to begin socializing the puppies and exposing them to new experiences to promote their development.

Breeding and giving birth to Dandie Dinmont Terriers is a serious responsibility, and should only be done by those who are committed to the health and well-being of the mother and her puppies. With proper care and attention, a Dandie Dinmont Terrier mother can give birth to healthy, happy puppies that will grow up to be loyal and loving companions.

Raising Dandie Dinmont Terrier Puppies

Raising Dandie Dinmont Terrier puppies requires a lot of patience, love, and attention. Here are some things to consider when raising a Dandie Dinmont Terrier puppy:

1. *Socialization: It's important to start socializing your Dandie Dinmont Terrier puppy early on, exposing them to different people, animals, and environments to help them develop good social skills. This can include taking them on walks, introducing them to other pets, and inviting friends and family members over to meet your new puppy.*

2. *Training: Training your Dandie Dinmont Terrier puppy is an essential part of raising a well-behaved adult dog. This can include house training, basic obedience training, and teaching them good manners. Positive reinforcement techniques, such as rewarding good behavior with treats and praise, can be very effective in training your Dandie Dinmont Terrier puppy.*

3. *Exercise: Dandie Dinmont Terriers are active dogs that require regular exercise to keep them healthy and happy. This can include daily walks, playtime in a fenced yard, and interactive toys that promote physical activity and mental stimulation.*

4. *Health care: It's important to take your Dandie Dinmont Terrier puppy to the veterinarian for regular check-ups, vaccinations, and preventative care. This can help catch any*

potential health issues early on and ensure that your puppy stays healthy and happy.

5. *Nutrition: Feeding your Dandie Dinmont Terrier puppy a healthy and balanced diet is essential for their growth and development. Consult with your veterinarian to determine the best type and amount of food to feed your puppy based on their age, weight, and activity level.*

Raising a Dandie Dinmont Terrier puppy can be a rewarding experience, but it requires a lot of time and effort. With proper socialization, training, exercise, health care, and nutrition, your Dandie Dinmont Terrier puppy can grow up to be a happy and healthy adult dog that is a beloved member of your family.

Socializing Dandie Dinmont Terrier Puppies

Socializing your Dandie Dinmont Terrier puppy is an essential part of raising a well-adjusted adult dog. Here are some tips for socializing your Dandie Dinmont Terrier puppy:

1. *Introduce your puppy to new people: Encourage your puppy to meet new people, including family members, friends, and strangers. Make sure that the people your puppy meets are friendly and gentle, and always supervise their interactions.*

2. *Introduce your puppy to other dogs: Allow your puppy to interact with other dogs in a safe and controlled environment, such as a dog park or obedience class. Make*

sure that the other dogs are well-behaved and friendly, and that your puppy is up to date on their vaccinations.

3. *Expose your puppy to new experiences: Introduce your puppy to new experiences, such as different sounds, smells, and environments. This can include taking them on car rides, walks in new neighborhoods, and visiting new places like pet stores and parks.*

4. *Reward good behavior: Praise and reward your puppy for good behavior, such as calmly meeting new people and dogs. Use treats and positive reinforcement to encourage your puppy to continue to behave well.*

5. *Be patient: Socializing your Dandie Dinmont Terrier puppy takes time and patience. Start early and be consistent, and remember that each puppy is different and may progress at their own pace.*

Socializing your Dandie Dinmont Terrier puppy is an important part of their development, and can help them become a well-adjusted adult dog. By introducing them to new people, dogs, and experiences, and rewarding good behavior, you can help your puppy grow into a confident and friendly companion.

Health Concerns for Dandie Dinmont Terrier Puppies

Like all dog breeds, Dandie Dinmont Terriers can be susceptible to certain health concerns, especially during their early years of life.

Here are some health concerns that Dandie Dinmont Terrier puppies may face:

1. *Hip dysplasia: This is a genetic condition that affects the hip joint, causing it to become misaligned or loose. Symptoms may include lameness, difficulty standing up or walking, and pain.*

2. *Eye problems: Dandie Dinmont Terriers can be prone to several eye problems, such as cataracts, glaucoma, and progressive retinal atrophy (PRA). These conditions can lead to vision loss and blindness.*

3. *Patellar luxation: This is a condition where the kneecap becomes dislocated, causing lameness and pain. It can be caused by genetics or trauma.*

4. *Thyroid problems: Dandie Dinmont Terriers can develop hypothyroidism, which is an underactive thyroid gland. This can lead to weight gain, lethargy, and skin problems.*

5. *Allergies: Some Dandie Dinmont Terriers may develop allergies to certain foods or environmental triggers, leading to skin irritation, itching, and ear infections.*

It's important to work closely with your veterinarian to ensure that your Dandie Dinmont Terrier puppy receives proper preventative care, including regular check-ups and vaccinations, to help prevent these health concerns from developing. Additionally, choosing a reputable breeder who screens their breeding dogs for these conditions can help minimize the risk of your puppy developing these health issues.

Training Dandie Dinmont Terrier Puppies

Training Dandie Dinmont Terrier puppies can be a rewarding experience, but it also requires patience and consistency. Here are some tips for training your Dandie Dinmont Terrier puppy:

1. *Start training early: The earlier you start training your Dandie Dinmont Terrier puppy, the easier it will be to teach them good habits and behaviors. Begin with basic obedience training such as sit, stay, come, and leash walking.*

2. *Use positive reinforcement: Dandie Dinmont Terriers are known to respond well to positive reinforcement training methods, such as using treats, praise, and toys as rewards. Avoid using punishment or physical corrections, as it can damage the trust between you and your puppy.*

3. *Socialize your puppy: Early socialization is important to help your Dandie Dinmont Terrier puppy become comfortable and confident around people, other dogs, and new situations. Expose your puppy to different environments, people, and other dogs in a positive and controlled way.*

4. *Be consistent: Consistency is key when it comes to training your Dandie Dinmont Terrier puppy. Use the same*

commands and rewards consistently, and enforce rules consistently. This will help your puppy understand what is expected of them.

5. *Keep training sessions short: Dandie Dinmont Terrier puppies have short attention spans, so it's important to keep training sessions short (around 10-15 minutes) and frequent throughout the day.*

6. *Seek professional help: If you're having trouble training your Dandie Dinmont Terrier puppy, consider seeking professional help from a certified dog trainer. They can provide personalized guidance and help you address specific behavior issues.*

Remember, training your Dandie Dinmont Terrier puppy should be a positive experience for both you and your puppy. Be patient, consistent, and use positive reinforcement to help your puppy learn and grow into a well-behaved and well-adjusted adult dog.

Competitions for Dandie Dinmont Terriers

Dandie Dinmont Terriers can participate in a variety of competitions that showcase their skills and abilities. Some popular competitions for Dandies include:

1. *Conformation shows: These shows evaluate the physical appearance and structure of the dog, and compare them to the breed standard.*

2. *Agility: This is a fast-paced, obstacle course-based competition that requires dogs to run, jump, and navigate through various obstacles.*

3. *Obedience: In obedience trials, dogs are judged on their ability to follow commands and perform specific tasks, such as heeling, retrieving, and staying.*
4. *Rally: Rally obedience is a more relaxed version of traditional obedience, with a course of signs that indicate different commands.*
5. *Earthdog trials: These tests evaluate a Dandie's instinctive ability to track and hunt small animals such as rats or rabbits.*
6. *Lure coursing: This is a competition that simulates the chase of live game, where dogs must follow a mechanically operated "lure" around a course.*

Competing in these events can be a fun and rewarding experience for both the Dandie Dinmont Terrier and their owner. It can also help to showcase the breed's unique abilities and talents.

Therapy and Service Work for Dandie Dinmont Terriers

Dandie Dinmont Terriers can make excellent therapy and service dogs due to their affectionate and loyal nature, as well as their intelligence and trainability.

Therapy dogs provide comfort and support to people in hospitals, nursing homes, schools, and other settings. Dandies can be trained to visit and interact with people who are elderly, ill, or experiencing emotional distress, providing a sense of companionship and joy.

Service dogs, on the other hand, are trained to assist people with disabilities and perform specific tasks to help them live more independently. Dandies can be trained as hearing or alert dogs to assist people with hearing impairments, or as mobility dogs to help people with physical disabilities.

In addition, Dandies can also be trained as search and rescue dogs, assisting in locating missing persons and providing aid in emergency situations.

To become a therapy or service dog, a Dandie Dinmont Terrier must undergo extensive training and socialization. They must also meet certain physical and temperament requirements to ensure they can safely and effectively perform their tasks.

Overall, therapy and service work can be a rewarding experience for both the Dandie Dinmont Terrier and their owner, as they work together to make a positive impact on the lives of others.

Hunting Background of Dandie Dinmont Terriers

The Dandie Dinmont Terrier has a strong hunting background, and was originally bred in Scotland for hunting otters and badgers. Their small size, strong jaws, and tenacious nature made them ideal for this type of work.

In the 18th and 19th centuries, otter hunting was a popular sport in the Scottish Borders region, and Dandies were highly prized for their ability to locate and chase otters into their dens. They would then stand guard at the den, preventing the otter from escaping, while their human handlers used nets or other tools to capture the otter.

In addition to otter hunting, Dandie Dinmont Terriers were also used for hunting small game such as rabbits and rats. Their compact size and ability to maneuver in tight spaces made them well-suited for this type of hunting.

Today, while otter hunting is no longer a popular sport, many Dandie Dinmont Terriers still retain their strong hunting instincts and enjoy activities such as earthdog trials, where they can demonstrate their natural abilities to locate and pursue small game.

It's important to note that while Dandies may have a strong hunting background, they also make loving and loyal family pets when provided with proper training, socialization, and exercise.

Fun Activities for Dandie Dinmont Terriers

Sure, here are some fun activities that Dandie Dinmont Terriers can enjoy:

1. *Agility training: This is a great way to keep your Dandie Dinmont Terrier physically and mentally active. It involves teaching your dog to navigate obstacles like tunnels, jumps, and weave poles.*

2. *Flyball: This high-energy sport involves a relay race with a team of dogs. Each dog must jump over a series of hurdles to retrieve a ball and then bring it back to their handler.*

3. *Tracking: Dandie Dinmont Terriers have a great sense of smell, making them well-suited for tracking activities. You can set up scent trails in your backyard or a nearby park for your dog to follow.*

4. *Rally obedience: This sport involves completing a series of obedience exercises in a timed course. It's a fun way to test your Dandie Dinmont Terrier's obedience skills.*

5. *Hiking: Dandie Dinmont Terriers love to explore the great outdoors. Take your dog on a hike and let them enjoy the sights and smells of nature.*

6. *Swimming: Many Dandie Dinmont Terriers enjoy swimming, and it's a great way to keep them cool and active in the summer months.*

7. *Playing fetch: A simple game of fetch can be a fun way to bond with your Dandie Dinmont Terrier and give them some exercise.*

8. *Puzzle toys: Dandie Dinmont Terriers are intelligent dogs, and they enjoy solving puzzles. You can find a variety of puzzle toys that will challenge your dog's mind and keep them entertained.*

Remember to always supervise your Dandie Dinmont Terrier during these activities and ensure that they are safe and appropriate for your dog's age and physical abilities.

Traveling with Dandie Dinmont Terriers

Traveling with a Dandie Dinmont Terrier can be a fun and rewarding experience, but it requires careful planning and preparation. Before embarking on a trip with your Dandie Dinmont Terrier, make sure you have all the necessary documents, such as vaccination records and a health certificate from your veterinarian.

When traveling by car, it's important to secure your Dandie Dinmont Terrier in a crate or with a seat belt harness to ensure their safety in case of an accident. Bring plenty of water and food for your dog, as well as any medications they may need. Take frequent breaks to allow your dog to stretch their legs and relieve themselves.

When traveling by air, make sure to choose a pet-friendly airline and book your dog's ticket well in advance. Check with the airline about their specific requirements for pet travel, such as crate size and health documentation. It's important to acclimate your Dandie Dinmont Terrier to their travel crate before the trip to reduce stress and anxiety.

No matter how you choose to travel with your Dandie Dinmont Terrier, always keep their safety and well-being in mind. With proper planning and preparation, traveling with your furry friend can be a fun and rewarding experience for both of you.

Living in Different Environments with Dandie Dinmont Terriers

Dandie Dinmont Terriers are adaptable to a wide range of living environments as long as they receive adequate exercise and attention. However, there are some considerations to keep in mind when living in different environments.

- *Apartment Living: Dandie Dinmont Terriers can do well in apartments as long as they receive daily exercise and playtime. They are not particularly noisy, but it's important to train them to not bark excessively.*

- *Suburban Living: Dandie Dinmont Terriers can thrive in suburban areas with a fenced yard. They enjoy exploring and playing, but it's important to supervise them as they may have a tendency to dig.*

- *Rural Living: Dandie Dinmont Terriers can enjoy living in rural areas, but it's important to keep them on a leash or in a fenced yard as they have a strong prey drive and may chase after small animals.*

- *Living with Children: Dandie Dinmont Terriers can do well with children as long as they are socialized and trained properly. They are sturdy and can tolerate rough play, but it's important to supervise interactions between children and dogs.*

- *Living with Other Pets: Dandie Dinmont Terriers can get along with other pets, but they may have a tendency to chase after small animals. It's important to supervise interactions and socialize them properly.*

Overall, Dandie Dinmont Terriers are adaptable and can thrive in a variety of living environments as long as they receive adequate attention, exercise, and training.

Living with Children and Dandie Dinmont Terriers

Living with children and Dandie Dinmont Terriers can be a great experience. Dandies are known for being friendly and gentle with children, and they often make great playmates. However, it's important to remember that every dog is an individual, and some may not be as tolerant of children as others.

If you have children and are considering getting a Dandie Dinmont Terrier, it's important to teach your children how to interact with dogs safely and respectfully. This includes teaching them to always approach dogs calmly and to ask permission before petting them. You should also supervise any interactions between your children and your Dandie Dinmont Terrier, especially when they are young.

Additionally, it's important to remember that Dandie Dinmont Terriers are small dogs and can be easily injured if they are mishandled. Teach your children to be gentle with your Dandie Dinmont Terrier and to never pull on their ears, tail, or fur.

Overall, Dandie Dinmont Terriers can make great family pets and can get along well with children if they are socialized properly and treated with respect.

Living with Other Pets and Dandie Dinmont Terriers

Dandie Dinmont Terriers can generally coexist peacefully with other pets if they are socialized properly from a young age. However, their strong prey drive can make them a danger to smaller animals such as birds or rodents, so caution should always be taken.

When it comes to living with other dogs, Dandie Dinmont Terriers can be selective about their canine companions. They may show aggression towards unfamiliar dogs, especially those of the same sex, but they can form close bonds with other dogs they are raised with.

Introducing a Dandie Dinmont Terrier to a new pet or dog should always be done gradually and under supervision. Proper socialization and training can help minimize any potential conflicts and ensure a peaceful coexistence.

Apartment Living with Dandie Dinmont Terriers

As a small breed, Dandie Dinmont Terriers can adapt well to apartment living. However, they still require daily exercise and mental stimulation to prevent boredom and destructive behavior. This can be accomplished through regular walks, playtime, and training sessions.

It is also important to provide a comfortable and safe living space for your Dandie Dinmont Terrier in your apartment. They will need a designated spot for their bed or crate, and access to fresh water and food. Regular grooming and cleaning will also be necessary to keep their living space and coat in good condition.

If you live in an apartment complex, it's important to follow the rules and regulations regarding pets. Some complexes may have breed or size restrictions, or require additional fees for having a pet. Additionally, it's important to be considerate of your neighbors and ensure your Dandie Dinmont Terrier doesn't disturb others with excessive barking or noise.

Made in United States
Cleveland, OH
02 November 2025

25160650R00030